AF483577

A HUMMINGBIRD RETURNS TO RAYPA

Peru, Pickleball, PSP, and My Life with Barney Myer

FRANCES A. MYER

A Hummingbird Returns to Raypa:
Peru, Pickleball, PSP, and My Life with Barney Myer

This is a memoir, and the events and experiences detailed in it have been presented as the author currently remembers them, to the best of her ability.

Published by Pickle Power Press
Kenmore, Washington

Author's email: pickleballstuff@gmail.com

Printed in the United States of America

ISBN (paperback): 979-8-218-47765-3
Library of Congress Control Number: 2024915309

Cover photo: The Central Plaza in Raypa, Peru, designed by Barney Myer.
Photo is courtesy of Rubén Paitan.
Cover design: Fran Myer
Interior design: Fran Myer

All photos are from the author's personal collection unless otherwise noted.

For the Myer family,
without them, this book would not have been written

CONTENTS

INTRODUCTION

As I looked out the window at my hummingbird feeder, I wondered when I would see another visitor. It had been weeks since I had seen any hummingbirds. Then, suddenly, as if on cue, a red-throated Anna's hummingbird stopped for several long sips of nectar. I thought about what little significance these birds held for me before meeting Barney. I had never seen one in person before that time, and I had only read about them in books. Now, their visits were special to me in a way I never imagined. They had become a sign that our world is full of wonder and mystery that is difficult to believe and even harder to explain.

Then I felt it. The need to tell the story about the fourteen extraordinary years I shared with Barney.

When I first met Barney, I was not looking for anyone to share my life. I was newly divorced, and in evaluating two failed marriages, I realized that I had become very independent and strong. I didn't need a man in my life to feel fulfilled or complete, plus I loved living by myself.

I was the youngest of two children, born in Seattle to Chinese American parents. My paternal grandmother lived with us and took care of my older brother and me. Since Ah Yun spoke very little English, Cantonese was my first language. She prepared all the dinners because both of my parents worked. We ate Chinese food almost every day. By age fourteen, I was assigned the task of cooking dinner—steamed rice, a light, broth-based soup with vegetables, several dishes of steamed or stir-fried meats or fish, and greens. We lived near Chinatown, in a neighborhood that was ethnically and culturally diverse. My uncle and aunt lived next door, and the streets surrounding our home were filled with many unrelated "aunties" and "uncles."

Barney and I appeared to be an unlikely couple. We had such different backgrounds as well as future goals. He came from a very religious family. I did not. He was looking for a relationship. I was not. He anticipated retirement in five or six years. I was on a very long road, with retirement many years away. However, our interest in a sport that was not well known at the time brought us together.

1

MEETING BARNEY MYER

In 1995, I had been playing pickleball for about seven years and signed up for one of Sid Williams's pickleball tournaments. A week before the event, I got a phone call from Sid. "I have a player who's looking for a mixed doubles partner. Do you want to do it?" I hesitated. "Think about it," he said.

Quickly, I assessed the situation. Here was a guy looking for a partner, and he obviously wasn't very picky, otherwise he would have asked for somebody with more experience. "Okay. Sign me up," I said.

"Great! Your partner's name is Barney Myer. Your first match will be at 5:30 on Friday."

Those were the early years of pickleball, a sport that combines elements of tennis, badminton, and table tennis. The game was invented by three dads one day in 1965 during a visit to their summer homes on Bainbridge Island, Washington. They wanted to create something to relieve their children's boredom. By the time I took up the sport, pickleball had gained a loyal following from a modest group of enthusiasts in the Pacific Northwest. Sid was the first executive director and president of the United States of America Pickleball Association (U.S.A.P.A.), and he was the only person putting on tournaments back then. Starting in 1984, he hosted these events every month or two in the Seattle-Tacoma area. They were marathon affairs, beginning after work on Fridays and continuing through the weekend. Matches could last until well past midnight, but there was always plenty of food for the players—hotdogs, chili, cookies, pretzels, and beer—all the ingredients for a great event. Competition was the best you could find for what was then a little-known sport, and it was always fun to meet other players.

Before pickleball, I'd only had brief introductions to bowling, tennis, and golf. Other than that, I wasn't involved in any type of sports or exercise except for seven years of classical ballet from ages five to twelve. After college, marriage, and three daughters, my schedule was filled with the responsibilities of being a parent and not so much on my own health. Following back surgery for a herniated disk in my early forties, I decided I needed to get into better shape. I had tried pickleball at a friend's house several years prior and it had been fun. More importantly, pickleball was an easy sport to learn, and almost anybody can enjoy playing after a five-minute introduction. Pickleball was going to get me into better physical shape. Unlike other sports that had classes, coaching, or other instruction, pickleball at that time was largely self-taught, with players bringing skills from other racquet sports and passing along helpful tips during play.

I started slowly with a group at the University of Washington (UW), where I worked. During my first year of playing, I was so out of shape that it sometimes felt like my arm was going to fly off when trying to hit the ball. Those under-developed muscles really needed strengthening. My sciatic nerve was still irritated from my herniated disk, so I had numbness and tingling in my right leg after a strenuous session. Gradually, my body got stronger, and the nerve sensations disappeared.

Soon I was going to local community centers during my lunch hour. Those venues were frequented by older, experienced players who were mostly very patient and helpful. They offered suggestions like hitting short, soft, controlled shots called "dinks" and hitting balls away from the opponents. (Yes, they actually had to tell me that.) It was slow going, but after several years, I began to play better. I was still a long way from being a good player, but I loved the activity and how it was improving my physical condition. Another benefit was meeting players of varied backgrounds.

Though I considered myself to be a little shy, introverted, and apprehensive about new experiences, my desire to improve gave me courage to visit new venues to play with different people. One incident convinced me my confidence was growing: At one gym, I encountered an elderly man, known for touching female players inappropriately, and I considered not going to play there any longer. Thoughts of this guy preventing me from enjoying my pickleball sessions at this location flipped a switch in me. Determined to put a stop to his objectionable behavior, I practiced in front of a mirror for several days. "If you touch me like that again, I'll . . . I'll . . ." Do what? After several tries, I came up with, "If you touch me like that again, I'll smack you where it'll hurt." I practiced shaking my pickleball paddle for extra emphasis. That was the best I could do, but it worked. He never bothered me again. That single confrontation gave me the self-assurance to challenge myself and to strive for more. *Should I try playing mixed doubles in a tournament?* Sure! Why not?

Barney and I met a few minutes before our first match. He was of medium height and looked very fit. His balding head and neatly trimmed mustache and beard were accented by dark-framed glasses that made his eyes look larger than they were. Strong, thin legs extended from the bottom of his red shorts. He looked to be around my age. "What's the best part of your game?" he asked.

I wasn't ready for this kind of probing question about my rather mediocre skills, but since we were about to play our first games together, it was a necessary query. "Well, I like running around a lot," I replied.

"Good. Because I have to have hip surgery soon and I'm not running very much right now."

I was a bit relieved by his response. It suggested that I might have something to bring to our partnership after all.

He was pleasant, easygoing, and athletic. We did not do well as a team—most likely due to my own lack of ability—but he was patient and not at all critical about my obvious shortcomings. I had this terrible fault of "popping the ball up," making an overhead smash coming back to my partner the predicted result. Too many times, I yelled, "Uh-oh!" to warn of the incoming missile (as if he could not see it coming) but I was never met with frustration, anger, or eye-rolling. The only thing worse than feeling like you've disappointed your partner is having them convey their impatience or exasperation. I felt great relief that Barney seemed just as pleasant after our matches as before.

As we walked off the court after our last game, he asked, "Where do you live?"

I was taken aback to be asked by this near stranger, so I gave a vague answer. "In the north end."

"Good! Can you give me a ride home?"

I mumbled something, indicating that I probably could, but I would have to check on something first. Barney seemed like a harmless, normal person, but childhood warnings about going off with strangers made me hesitant. I casually walked over to the tournament desk where Sid was busy organizing match results and announcing the next group. Hoping to get affirmation that Sid knew Barney well enough to vouch for his character, I said, "Barney asked me to give him a ride home."

Sid looked up briefly, responded with an enthusiastic "Great!" and went back to his score sheets.

That wasn't exactly the affirmation I was seeking, but my instincts told me it would be okay, and at least Sid would know who I was with if I suddenly went missing.

The 17-mile drive to Barney's house was uneventful. The conversation was not awkward but also not particularly personal. I was not in the habit of revealing much about myself to someone I didn't know. Barney explained that he usually carpooled to his job at Sea-Tac Airport, a short distance from the tournament venue. He found somebody to give him a ride from work to the gym, but getting home required finding someone who lived in the north part of Seattle who was willing to give him a ride. It didn't seem like a very solid plan to me, but here I was, driving this near stranger to somewhere "in the north end." Surprisingly, out of the vastness of North Seattle, I dropped Barney off at his house less than a mile from my own home. I briefly thought to myself what a strange coincidence that was, but soon my busy life took over and I thought very little of this first encounter after that.

2

THE FIRST DATE

I didn't see Barney again for over two years until I decided to sign up for the Seattle Senior Games, for players fifty and older. Participants only compete against those in their specific five-year age group. Prior to the tournament I received a call from Nikki Ryan, the event's commissioner. She had a guy in my age group who was looking for a mixed doubles partner. His name? Barney Myer. *Oh good*, I thought. *It's the guy who doesn't get upset when I pop up the ball.* I agreed to the partnership, feeling that I could count on a stress-free experience. Again, the games we played were fine but did not exactly set the pickleball world on fire.

After the Seattle Senior Games, we again went our separate ways. By now, I had played mixed doubles in several tournaments with different partners, and I simply considered Barney an occasional partner for pickleball. Nothing more.

With very few pickleball venues in those early years, players would often share locations, days, and times of places to play. I learned that a gym on Mercer Island had pickleball on Sunday evenings. It fit nicely into my schedule. The players were friendly and had pickleball skills that were challenging but not completely outside my level of play. Often, Barney was there as well.

Given that Barney knew I lived somewhere in the north part of Seattle, he suggested we carpool on Sundays to save gas and money. Saving money was on my mind as well.

In addition to my full-time job at the UW as a fiscal specialist, I was a weekend receptionist at a real estate office, and I worked the graveyard shift at a data services company one night per week. I was also a bookkeeper for a restaurant. I worked seven days a week, which by this time had been my schedule for about seven years. Sometime during one of my marriages, when things were not going so well, my husband suggested that a divorce would most likely result in my having to go live with my mother. That scenario was totally unacceptable to me. It signified utter failure. Though my one job at the UW was adequate, each extra job was added insurance against that dire prediction. My grand plan was to pay off my mortgage by the time I retired at age sixty-seven. Then I could collect my pension from the UW as well as my Social Security and enjoy a reasonably secure retirement. Only fourteen more years to go. I had my sights set resolutely on my goal, and without diversions (except for pickleball), I was going to make my plan work.

Weeks of carpooling went by, and the two of us got better acquainted during those Sunday car rides. We talked about our children, and work, but most of our conversations were related to pickleball. One day, Barney asked why my husband didn't also play pickleball.

"Husband?"

"Yeah. Every time I call, I get a message saying I've reached Fran and Bob," Barney replied.

"Oh. I don't have a husband. I have that on my voice message so men won't bother me." That message was mainly for safety reasons—so that callers wouldn't think I lived alone. I knew that Barney was divorced, but I hoped my response would somehow communicate that I was not looking for a relationship.

My two divorces had been instructive. They'd told me that marriage was not necessarily the right thing for me. At this point in my life, taking care of myself was all the challenge I wanted or needed. My three daughters were grown and out of the house. With my nose to the grindstone, I was determined to get to my retirement goal. Pickleball was a fun activity that I could enjoy during the few free hours I had, and it kept me physically fit.

Carpooling with Barney continued. On Sunday, February 20, 2000, as we were driving home from pickleball, Barney invited me into his house for a drink of mango juice. My heavy work schedule did not allow for much socializing, so I welcomed the opportunity to visit for a while. The conversation flowed easily and there was something very appealing about Barney's humble, easygoing nature and self-confidence.

As he showed me around his house, I was impressed with his handywork and tiling skills. It was a chilly night, so Barney lit a fire in his fireplace. It created a warmth that made it feel safe to let down my guard and share more about my background and life. As our conversation continued, I was struck by how much Barney reminded me of my dad, a man who had the patience of a Taoist priest, who was caring, understanding, kind, and always helping people. Dad had been gone for over nineteen years at that point, but I still missed his loving, gentle, positive presence.

Shortly after the mango juice on Sunday, Barney invited me to dinner. I was a bit surprised, since nothing in our previous interactions indicated "Let's go to dinner sometime." With my busy schedule, going out to dinner with anyone for any reason was a rarity. But how could I refuse someone who was so much like my beloved dad? I accepted the invitation.

On the way to the restaurant, Barney said he needed to stop at the car dealership because he was buying a new truck.

This seemed a little out of the ordinary for a dinner date, but I followed him into the showroom where he met with a salesman. Apparently, Barney had made all the arrangements ahead of time and assumed he could go in, write a check, and leave with the truck after a few minutes. There was a minor problem. The dealership wanted to put Barney on a credit plan. Barney insisted that he didn't want to pay with credit. He was going to write a check. Mr. Thrifty Guy was not going to pay interest on credit!

If I learned anything from our carpool conversations, it was that Barney was very careful with his spending. Gas was from the least expensive pumps. Nothing in his house was extravagant. When he needed a quick meal, he purchased a footlong Subway sandwich—but only when there was a special. They had a wide selection of toppings, of which he selected almost all. Splitting these sandwiches in half meant he could have two meals, each for one-half of the sale price.

An hour turned into two hours as the situation tried to work itself out. At one point, the credit manager invited Barney to his office in the back. Barney had been holding his checkbook, poised to write the check, so he handed it to me while he went to the office. Sitting there with nothing to do, I glanced at the checkbook and saw the name at the top: "Harold L. Myer." *Harold? Who is Harold?* I puzzled over why Barney was paying for his truck from Harold L. Myer's checking account. Finally, I reasoned that Barney must really be Harold. But how did he get from Harold to Barney? It gave me something to ponder as I waited.

Three hours after arriving at the dealership, Barney closed the deal and was given the keys. He promptly handed them to me and said, "You get to drive the new truck while I drive the car and we'll meet at the restaurant."

"Noooo!" I protested. I was not going to drive somebody else's brand-new truck off the dealership lot and worry about crashing into something, especially on a first date! *Who is this guy? And who is Harold?* At Barney's insistence, I ended up driving his new truck, gripping the steering wheel with anxiety as I made my way 2 miles to the restaurant.

Barney was different from anybody I'd ever met. I had a feeling that getting to know him was going to be very interesting.

3

BECOMING BARNEY MYER

Early in our friendship, I often heard Barney speaking Spanish with his brother. They were clearly fluent, but his parents were not. I was curious to learn how that came about. Over the years, stories were shared, and conversations with other family members allowed me to combine all the details into an understanding of the Myer family background.

Barney was the son of Everett and Miriam (née Larson) Myer. Everett Burr Myer was born in Indiana on July 29, 1914, to Charles Isaac and Tressa May (née Burr) Myer. Everett was the oldest of eight children. The family moved from Manchester, Indiana, to Sunnyside, Washington, in the 1920s, where Everett completed his pre-college schooling. After high school, Everett attended La Verne College in Southern California. After receiving his bachelor's degree, he went on to study medicine at the College of Medical Evangelists of Loma Linda, now known as Loma Linda University. Loma Linda was a Seventh-day Adventist school and at the time allowed only one non-SDA medical student per class. The year that Everett started medical school, he was that one student.

Miriam Larson was born in Edmonton, Alberta, Canada, on November 25, 1914, to Hilner Nickolas Larson and Kristofa Jacobson. Kristofa passed away in 1917 at the age of twenty-six from generalized peritonitis when Miriam was two and a half. Within a year of Kristofa's death, Hilner married Elizabeth A. Barstow. Together they had a son named Edwin.

After high school, Miriam attended Portland Adventist Sanitarium and Hospital School of Practical Nursing in Oregon. After completing her studies in Oregon, Miriam went to Loma Linda in California. Everett and Miriam met when she was a charge nurse at Loma Linda's Obstetrics and Gynecology Department. They were married on April 4, 1941, in Long Beach, California.

After medical school, Everett went to work as a newly trained doctor at the building site of the Shasta Dam in California. Near the end of his three years there, he and Miriam welcomed their first son, Ralph Edwin, in 1944. Everett and Miriam had made plans to live their lives as missionaries, with Everett devoting his medical services to the missionary field. Initially, they were assigned to go to Africa. In anticipation of their travel there, they sold all their belongings and had their baggage and personal items shipped. They were ready to leave when word came that those plans were cancelled. Due to World War II, many civilian ships crossing the Atlantic had been under attack from German submarines. Going to Africa was now deemed too dangerous. All their baggage and personal items were gone, never to be returned to them. They gathered what they could and went on to their new assignment in Castañer, a small inland village located in the western half of Puerto Rico. There, Everett served as a medical missionary in the Church of the Brethren's Castañer Hospital. They arrived when Ralph Edwin was just a few months old. As one of a handful of doctors in Castañer, Everett delivered their second son, Harold Lewis, on September 3, 1946. Two years later, he delivered their first daughter, Jeanne Elizabeth.

After returning to the US in 1949, Dr. Myer received surgical training in Boston from 1950 to 1951. That was followed in 1953 by an assignment to the American Baptist Hospital Latino Americano in Puebla, Mexico. This is where young Harold spent his childhood from ages seven to fourteen.

Upon their arrival in Puebla, the family was provided with living quarters within the hospital. The children were enrolled in the Colegio Americano de Puebla (American School), located a little more than a mile from the hospital. Being unfamiliar with Spanish when the family arrived, Harold was required to repeat first grade. Ralph was placed in fourth grade on a trial basis and stayed there the entire year. Jeanne entered kindergarten. The children quickly adjusted to bilingual life, with English spoken at home and Spanish at school. The schoolteachers were from both the US and Mexico—each teaching in their native language. It became second nature for the children to switch back and forth between English and Spanish, depending on which teacher was leading the class.

I learned in conversations with Barney and Ed that their family did not have much while living in Mexico, but they couldn't recall being short on toys or in need of anything. They had the usual teddy bears, coloring books, puzzles, and board games. The boys were given a bike, which was quite a luxury. They would ride the bike together to and from school. Ralph would do all the pedaling since he was bigger and had longer legs, while Harold sat on an attached seat behind Ralph. Every afternoon after school, Ralph would meticulously clean and care for the bike.

The children often amused themselves by playing hide-and-seek in their living quarters of the hospital, sometimes with the lights out for added excitement. On occasion, they would expand their hiding area to include parts of the actual hospital, much to the disapproval of their father.

Miriam made sure they all had clean clothes to wear. She had a washing machine with rollers to squeeze out the excess water. She would lug all the wet laundry up three flights of stairs to hang on the rooftop clothesline. She ironed everything except their socks. All water was boiled, and food was prepared with great care to prevent being infected with parasitic amoeba or salmonella. They all took anti-parasitic medication once a year to clear up any undetected infections.

Many of Dr. Myer's patients could not afford to pay for treatments. Instead of cash, they sometimes brought chickens, eggs, or avocados. Ralph (who used the name Ed as an adult) recounted a time when a patient invited the Myer family to his place out in the "country boondocks." They had to take unpaved roads that were so rough that his dad had to stop the car frequently and order everyone out so he could drive over obstructions without scraping the bottom of the vehicle. Upon arrival, Dr. Myer commented on the nice apricots growing on a tree near the country house. After being served a meal with exceedingly spicy *mole* (pronounced "mo-lay"—a traditional sauce used in Mexican cuisine), the Myers were presented with several boxes of apricots. The patient's family had picked every apricot from the tree that Dr. Myer had admired. They also gave him a small bag of red beans, which were the biggest red beans Ralph had ever seen.

After the family welcomed baby sister Susan Tressa in August 1956, they remained in Mexico for four more years before returning to the US in 1960. They settled in Okanogan, a small town in the northeastern part of Washington state with a population of less than two thousand. Ralph had been attending Southwestern Academy and Junior College in Keene, Texas, and did not join the family until he completed the school year. Harold quickly assimilated into American life and adjusted well. His ninth-grade Okanogan yearbook shows that he was voted "Most Popular" student that year. The following year, he started tenth grade at Okanogan High School, which had about 250 students at that time. Harold did well in his academic subjects and also participated in football and track.

In 1962, Harold started working for Claud Gann during the summer months. Claud owned a construction company that built homes and businesses throughout Okanogan County. During eight summers of working with Claud, Harold learned building and construction skills, as well as carpentry. During one job, he was a hod carrier (a worker who uses a V-shaped open trough on a pole to carry building materials). One day, as he was climbing a ladder to deliver bricks, something caused the ladder to shift. The bricks were flung to the side, and young Harold was knocked to the ground, unconscious. His father was called to the scene, and after one look at his son, he said, "Take him to the hospital." Thankfully, there were no lasting injuries, and Harold quickly returned to work.

Harold finished high school in 1965 and entered La Verne College, his dad's and older brother Ralph's alma mater. Although they were only two years apart in age, due to Harold being held back a year in Mexico and Ralph skipping the tenth grade, Ralph had fast-tracked himself through his academic programs and was already in the middle of his own medical school pursuits.

During his first few days of orientation at La Verne, Harold went to the sports fields to see if he could participate in some activities. Suddenly, somebody yelled, "Barney! We need another guy out there!" Looking around to see who they were talking to, he noticed their finger pointing at him. "Yeah—you, Barney! Get out there!" From that point on, fellow students called him Barney. The following year when he transferred to Washington State University (WSU), letters from friends at La Verne, addressed to "Barney Myer," were announced during mail call. "Letter for Barney Myer! Letter for Barney Myer!" And so, the name stuck.

The Myer family in 1965
Back row, L-R: Ralph (Ed), Everett, Harold (Barney)
Front row, L-R: Jeanne, Miriam, Susan

4

COLLEGE AND BEYOND

During Barney's college years, the US was in the midst of the very unpopular Vietnam War. Although male university students were granted temporary deferment from military service, they were subject to the draft once they left school or graduated. It was a time of unrest as anti-war protests took place on many college campuses. Conscientious objectors, draft card burnings, and teach-ins were all part of college life. There was great incentive to study hard and stay in school.

While at WSU, Barney became friends with Pollard Dickson, an older student who had completed military service before entering WSU as a Navy veteran. They were fellow students in the architecture program. Pollard described Barney as one of the more serious and talented architectural students with a gift for brilliant design: "He was the brightest and best student in our class bar none." They maintained a close friendship throughout their years at WSU and beyond. In 1969, Barney graduated with distinction, earning a bachelor's degree in architecture.

Due to the Myer family's religious convictions against war activities, after graduation Barney went to Peru for three years as an alternative to his US military obligations. He helped to rebuild towns and villages that had been decimated by the great Peruvian earthquake of 1970. Projects began in Huarmey near the coast. This was followed by work in Aija, Sucha, and Raypa, all remote villages in parts of the Andes where there was no electricity or running water. Ed (Ralph) visited Barney in Aija for a short time and recalled that dinner was a five-course meal made entirely of potatoes prepared in various manners. In fact, during Barney's entire time in Aija, he ate nothing but potatoes. Despite the difficult conditions and limited food resources,

Barney would look back on this experience as his most memorable and where he felt he had achieved his life's greatest accomplishments.

After his time in Peru, Barney returned to the US. In 1973, he attended graduate school at Kansas State University, studying regional and community planning for one and a half semesters. While there, he was a graduate teaching assistant and the sole instructor for the undergraduate graphics class. His graduate studies at KSU ended when he was offered an internship that he could not turn down.

In 1938, the US Army Corps of Engineers completed the Bonneville Lock and Dam, located 40 miles east of Portland, Oregon, on the Columbia River. It was the first federal project of this type to be constructed. Its purpose was to generate power for the Pacific Northwest and provide for the safe navigation of ships around the Cascades Rapids. Drawings of the original plan showed a second powerhouse to be constructed in the exact area occupied by the town of North Bonneville, Washington. The timeline for this project was vague, and the five hundred residents of this town were in a constant state of anxiety, waiting for the plans to be verified and acted upon. After many years of anticipation, federal agencies confirmed this to be the site for the second powerhouse, and the Corps started making plans without a precise timeline. In an effort to take control of their own destiny, the townspeople began meeting to chart their future. There was never any question that they wanted to be relocated as a town as opposed to being bought out individually and dispersed. They looked everywhere for help and funding. Finally, in 1972, the town asked for help from Russell Fox, a planner and faculty member at The Evergreen State College in Olympia, Washington. Fox had created an unusual urban planning project with a group of students who worked in the field under an arrangement with the college. Barney's friend Pollard Dickson was one of Fox's students. He had gone back to school to gain more experience in planning. Pollard and a handful of fellow

20

students decided to take on the North Bonneville assignment. After initial visits and preliminary reviews, Pollard became the planning coordinator of the relocation project. He thought Barney would be a valuable member of the team. At Pollard's invitation, Barney left his KSU program in 1974 and headed to North Bonneville to join them. Barney worked as the senior planner with the City of North Bonneville. From 1974 to 1975, he helped create plans to relocate the city.

I asked Pollard to tell me, in his own words, about Barney's contribution:

By living in the town and listening to what the people there envisioned for their new home, Barney was able to translate their inputs into design criteria for construction of a new town. Barney's skill set with his degree in architecture from Washington State University, coupled with his living experiences in Peru helping to rebuild a community devastated by a massive mudslide, provided the group with essential technical language needed for writing a scope of work for the design of their new town. Barney's contribution, because of his ability to listen to the people, gave them an understanding of design criteria needed for design and construction of their new town. His ability to work with the people, the planning team, and the local government rein-forced the group's ability to fill the needs of the town and preserve their way of life.

Barney married Mary Lynne in December 1974. She had a young daughter, Heidi, from a previous relationship. The three of them lived together in North Bonneville during the relocation project. After completing his work with the City of North Bonneville, Barney turned his attention back to his advanced studies. He entered the University of Washington, and in 1978 he received his master's degree in urban planning. That same year, Mary Lynne gave birth to their son, Eric.

Barney's next major project took him to Fairbanks, Alaska. In 1982, while working as a consulting urban planner for Wilsey Ham, Barney helped develop the Comprehensive Land Use Plan for the Fairbanks North Star Borough. Accompanied by his family, Barney spent a year in Fairbanks working on the master plan, which was presented in August 1983. The plan was subsequently adopted in 1984.

After returning from Alaska, Barney went to work for the Port of Seattle. Starting in 1983, he worked in several different departments on projects such as the Noise Remedy Program. His work in the facilities section involved developing new construction, planning remodels and maintenance projects in cooperation with the Engineering Department. He also worked on the high-capacity transit connections to the airport. He stayed with the Port of Seattle until his retirement in 2005 as Project Manager/Senior Planner in the Aviation Project Management Group. The last project he worked on was the expansion of the Central Terminal at Seattle-Tacoma International Airport.

5
WHAT A YEAR

Pickleball was the theme of Barney and my relationship. By mid-2000, Barney and I began seeing each other more seriously. I had started Pickleball Stuff LLC, an online business selling equipment and supplies for the sport of pickleball. While at my weekend job at the real estate office, I had very little to occupy my time in between answering phones and filing. They just needed a warm body in case the phones rang. My boss told me to fill my time by reading magazines or playing video games. Instead, I decided to use this free time to create a website about this game that had become my passion: pickleball.

It began as an informational site about the sport, with pages about the history of pickleball, how to create courts, and where to play. It soon took on a life of its own as people began asking where they could purchase equipment and supplies. After several months of directing them to the two manufacturers that existed at the time, it occurred to me that if I had the "stuff," they could buy it from me. That is how Pickleball Stuff became the first online retail site for pickleball. I was able to obtain paddles on consignment and get business cards for free from an internet special offer. The website was also free, so I was able to start my retail business without investing a single penny.

Looking back, it must have been a very busy time—with my full-time job at the UW, three part-time jobs, and now an online business.

Before long, Barney encouraged me to quit some of my four jobs. "Why?" I asked.

"I never get to see you because you're always working," he answered.

Perhaps he was right. At the time, Pickleball Stuff was the only online presence selling pickleball equipment, and things were starting to pick up. Gradually, I gave up all the part-time jobs, leaving only my full-time position at the University of Washington's Center for Urban Horticulture (CUH) and my growing online business. Barney willingly helped me process orders. Several times a week, in the evenings, we would package up pickleball supplies together.

In July 2000, Barney became an official partner in my business. As a partner, he could finally voice his concerns over my business model. We shipped all orders without prior payment. The invoice would be tucked inside the package with a return envelope for payment to be sent back to us. I told all our customers that if they liked their "stuff" to please send us a check. If they didn't like it, they could return the items with no questions asked. It was very old fashioned, but I trusted people's honesty, and in return we had many customers tell us how much they appreciated being trusted. One customer who was late with his payment added his own late fee. Another customer who was late with his payment sent us a beautiful coffee table book on architecture and a note of apology. In all the years of having the business, we never lost more than .01 percent in a year due to nonpayment. This was much less than the percentage we would have lost through credit card payment fees, so after several years, I was able to convince Barney that my business model was financially sound.

During the first year of being business partners and acknowledging ourselves as a couple, we spent time meeting family members and getting to know them better. Barney's daughter, Heidi, had finished college and was now married to Jack. They were living in Seattle, and there were many opportunities to see them. Barney's son, Eric, was close to finishing his bachelor's degree at Western Washington University in Bellingham, so visits with him were not as frequent but happened when schedules allowed. The kids were all easy to be around. I was relieved and happy for what felt like warm acceptance of me in their dad's life.

In June, Barney invited me to Okanogan Days to see friends and acquaintances from his high school years. Along the way, Barney and I picked up his sister Jeanne in Wenatchee. It was my first time meeting her. Without my prior knowledge, she and Barney had arranged for the three of us to share a hotel room. I gave a sideways glance, shrugged my shoulders, and went with the flow.

The next morning at the town's outdoor pancake breakfast, we met Barney's parents, Everett and Miriam (Ev and Mim), as well as his sister Sue and her husband, Mark. I watched with amusement as each family member came by to make sure Mim had everything she needed. Without realizing somebody else had already helped her, each one picked up the maple syrup and painted a generous circle on Mim's stack of pancakes. By the time she started to eat, each bite was fully saturated with yummy, sweet goodness.

Shortly after breakfast, we all gathered along the main street to watch the parade. This was my first experience being in a small town, and I was treated to the quaint charm of it. City officials and dignitaries came riding down the few blocks of the parade route—each in a neatly polished vehicle—followed by a variety of farm machinery, people on horses, fire trucks, and finally concluding with a flatbed truck featuring residents from the town's retirement facility. They each sat in wheelchairs separated by bales of hay. Everyone applauded—a nice tribute to the senior citizens of this little town.

We took a drive past the house where the Myer family once lived, and to the town of Omak, less than 5 miles away, to see the clinic where Dr. Myer had worked after the family moved here from Mexico. The high school hosted a program later in the afternoon. The day ended with dinner at the home of Barney's old high school employer, Claud Gann. He and his wife, Alverna, had a beautiful hilltop home that provided a 360-degree view of the town and surrounding area. The trip gave me insight into Barney's early years. It was strange to hear him referred to as Harold by those who knew him before his college transformation to Barney. It also gave me a firsthand glimpse into the life of the Myer family and their close bond.

In September, we went to Spokane for his niece's wedding, and this time we shared a room with Ed. I gave another sideways glance. "My family does everything together," Barney explained. Underlying all this togetherness was the cost-saving benefit of shared quarters, which I presumed was the result of growing up with so little.

In getting to know more family members, I learned that Ed was especially careful with his finances. Never married, and a longtime physician in family medicine, he was legend in the family for being super thrifty. Barney times ten. Stories about Ed's frugality were often accompanied by a sigh, a slow shake of the head, or utter disbelief.

In the colder months, it was not unusual to find Ed fully dressed in a jacket and hat while walking around in his unheated house—heat costs money. Lights were turned on only when necessary, and if he knew you were coming to visit, that still was not reason enough to turn on a light. Ed also had a habit of collecting rainwater that he then used to flush his toilets, thus conserving water as well as saving on his water bills. Navy showers were his routine for the same reason.

Like other family members, I would come to regard Ed with respect and appreciation for his genuine concern for others and his ultralight footprint on our planet's resources.

In October, Barney and I flew to San Diego to visit my middle daughter, Diane. My oldest daughter, Alex, her husband, and their one-year-old son, had flown in from New York. Other family members and friends joined us throughout the few days we were there. Since Alex's move to New York six years before, gatherings with her had been very infrequent, so the time in San Diego with her, my grandson, and other family members was a real treat. I was also glad for the opportunity to introduce everyone to Barney. We had a relaxing time walking the beach, seeing the sights, and taking in the beautiful sunsets.

Just prior to our San Diego trip, Barney had moved in with me. We were spending more time together, and with the growing pickleball business, we were also spending more time working together from my home-based living room warehouse. The start of the school year was also an ideal time to find renters for his now-vacant house.

We settled into a great routine of work, pickleball, work, and more pickleball. Any apprehensions I may have had about living with someone were totally unfounded. Our transition to housemates was without stress. Barney was easy to live with. He willingly shared housework, which even included scrubbing the toilets. Those gleaming white toilet bowls completely won my heart. We continued to play in tournaments—sometimes as partners in mixed doubles. As my game improved, we started to have more pickleball successes both individually and as a team.

In November, we helped Barney's parents move from their condo to a nearby assisted-living apartment in Wenatchee, Washington. That same month, in Seattle, my mother suffered a massive stroke. It left her entirely disabled and in need of nursing home care. Our parents were going through changes and challenges. We were unaware that it was just the beginning of a twelve-month period that would be filled with life-altering events.

We welcomed 2001 with a series of parties and gatherings. Trips to the nursing home to attend to my mother's needs punctuated my weekly routine while I maintained my work schedule and ran our business. At the end of February, the Seattle area was hit with the Nisqually earthquake. The 6.8 temblor was one of the largest recorded earthquakes in Washington and caused damage all around Seattle. The control tower at Sea-Tac Airport was damaged severely enough to reroute air traffic for several hours. Barney came home from work that evening with a chunk of the shattered control tower window. The inch-thick glass was silent testimony to the power of the quake. Though over four hundred injuries were reported, only one person's heart-attack death was attributed to the event. Seattle went into repair mode to fix several billion dollars in damages.

In the months that followed, my travel plans took me through Sea-Tac, and I could see firsthand the ongoing work being done at the airport. For Barney, his work environment bore daily reminders of the earthquake's potency. Though the only structural damage was sustained by the control tower, there was extensive nonstructural damage throughout the terminal caused by water, falling ceiling tiles, cracked walls, and broken light fixtures. Different areas were walled off each time we walked through the terminal as progress was made to complete all the repairs.

On the morning of May 21, I headed to the Center for Urban Horticulture at the UW to start my workday. I was unaware of the events that had occurred overnight. Upon arrival I was met with fire engines, police cars, reporters, and grief-stricken faculty and staff standing outside our burned-out building. Ecoterrorists had firebombed the office of a biology professor who occupied the space next to mine. The building was a complete loss. The fire destroyed precious research papers, records, slides, rare plant samples, books, computers, and lab equipment. Trailers were brought in to temporarily house some of the staff. I was assigned a small cubicle space in the greenhouse along with the director, administrative assistant, and plant propagator. The rebuilding of CUH would take almost four years at a cost of $5.4 million.

The year was presenting us with challenges, but despite all the disruptions at work, our schedules were still filled with lots of gatherings and activities. Barney and I agreed to be the pickleball commissioners for the Washington State Senior Games, a task we would assume for a total of nine years. We encouraged Barney's eighty-seven-year-old dad to come and compete in table tennis. When the family lived in Mexico, Ev had played a lot of *frontenis*, a racquet sport created in Mexico in 1900 and played on *pelota* courts. His competitive spirits awakened when he faced his opponent at the table tennis event that day. He battled and won the gold medal, much to our family's delight.

Barney and I settled into a wonderful partnership on all fronts while progress was made restoring our workplaces. We had plans to visit Alex and her husband in New York at the beginning of October to celebrate our grandson's second birthday. More pickleball tournaments were scheduled for the remainder of the year. Pickleball Stuff was continuing to grow. Our relationship felt very natural, compatible, loving, and secure. We were in a happy place.

After the CUH firebombing, I developed the habit of turning on the TV news each morning—fearful of missing anything important. On the morning of September 11, the TV was on as Barney and I got ready for work. It took several minutes for us to grasp what was actually happening. As the horror of the events began to sink in, my concern immediately turned to Alex, who was working in Manhattan.

Though a safe distance away, she was able to see the scene unfold from the vantage of her office. Two commercial passenger planes, hijacked by terrorists, had deliberately crashed into each of the World Trade Center towers—two of the world's five tallest buildings at that time. Fire immediately engulfed both buildings, and within two hours, they had completely collapsed. The entire area turned to chaos as people tried to leave the stricken city and find their way out. Alex emailed the family, telling us that no subways were running, bridges were closed, and many had to walk to escape Manhattan. People were climbing fences and hopping over medians to reach their destinations. The bridge Alex walked across had a sea of people both in the car lanes and pedestrian walkways. People were loaning money for phone calls or other emergencies; some were letting strangers get into their cars and taking them wherever they needed to go. New Yorkers were at their best, helping one another during a massive crisis. Much to my relief, Alex made it home safely, but the trauma would continue for a very long time, as many waited to learn the fate of their loved ones.

Sea-Tac Airport quickly put new safety protocols in place, and Barney's work world changed once again. I worried about our planned trip to New York, but Barney assured me that things were safe.

On October 4, we flew to New York. The events of 9/11 had reduced passenger travel significantly, so we went through security quickly. Upon landing at JFK, the first hint of change was the armed military personnel surveying passengers in the terminal. It was hard to ignore the tragedy of the prior month's events. Even as we stepped outside Alex's apartment in Brooklyn Heights, the smell of burnt electrical wire and dust from the collapsed towers remained in the air. A walk along the Brooklyn Heights Promenade gave us a view of the lower Manhattan skyline. On the fence, somebody had hung a large framed picture of the skyline taken prior to 9/11. In the picture, from this same location, you could clearly see the two World Trade Center towers—now gone.

We walked across the Brooklyn Bridge to get a glimpse of the large, gaping hole where cleanup operations were in full swing. I was struck by the resilience of New Yorkers. In little more than three weeks, workers were carrying on with business as usual. Restaurants and delis were serving up meals in normal fashion. We visited the Botanical Garden, took in a show, and celebrated my grandson's birthday as if nothing was out of the ordinary. However, the tremendous number of casualties could not be ignored as we stopped by some of the numerous makeshift memorials in front of fire stations and other places around town. It was so very sad—a sadness that is still hard to put into words.

After our New York trip, we returned to work and a busy schedule of activities. We visited family in Wenatchee and Spokane, played pickleball, and attended several dinner parties. Andrea, a friend from my childhood, came from Sacramento to Seattle for a visit. We arranged with Wanda and Marilyn, two other longtime friends, to have a slumber party. We chose an upscale, funky hotel in downtown Seattle that offered us a companion goldfish for the night. It had been many years since the four of us had gotten together, and we had fun sharing news about our families and friends. After my girls' weekend, Barney wanted to know what we did. "We talked a lot and caught up on family and friends," I said.

"What else?" Barney asked.

"Well, Andrea wanted to know when we're going to get married," I replied.

"We should talk about it," said Barney.

That was it. No trail of red rose petals leading to a surprise proposal or romantic candlelit dinner ending with the presentation of a beautiful ring and "the question."

"Yes. We should talk about it."

Barney's first gift to me was an electric toothbrush. It was nothing fancy, but it was something I needed and appreciated. The gift of a toothbrush was a bit like our relationship—thoughtful, practical, and functional. In the same vein, our parents' age-related health issues had motivated us (with Ed's strong suggestion) to enroll ourselves in a joint long-term care policy. At the time, Barney delighted in one of the benefits: unmarried couples with a joint policy could get paid to care for one another. But this would not apply if the couple was married. It was now a benefit we didn't mind losing—definitely a sign of our love. We had become partners in Pickleball Stuff during the previous year, so this businesslike approach to taking the next step seemed logical and inevitable. Even without the rose petals, we were both giddy, thrilled, and excited for the future. It was a great way to put a positive exclamation point on a year that had been filled with grief, horror, destruction, and changes. What a year it had been.

6

A PICKLEBALL WEDDING

"What day should we get married?" Barney asked.

I thought for a few moments. "I know! Let's get married on the same day you invited me in for mango juice. That's how this all got started. And this is great—next year, that date will be 02-20-2002."

We laughed and thought what a wonderful date that would be.

We started to work on the details. Suddenly, we both realized that we had plans for that date. We were signed up to play in the Arizona Senior Olympics (ASO) and would be competing together in the mixed doubles event. We did a little research and found that we could get a marriage license in Wickenburg, north of the tournament location in Surprise. We just had to make sure the schedule that day would end early enough for us to get to the Wickenburg Town Court before their 5:30 closing time. We were friends with Earl Hill, the ASO commissioner, so we called to find out the schedule for that day's matches. "Why do you need to know?" he asked. After we explained our situation, Earl said he would call us back with more information. Sure enough, a short time later, he called. "Why don't you guys get married on the pickleball court during the tournament?"

"No" was my immediate reaction. People were coming from all around the country to compete, not to attend a wedding. But Earl was persuasive, insisting that it would be a big plus for the tournament. After going back and forth for a bit, Barney and I finally agreed.

"Do you guys have a budget for your wedding?" asked Earl.

"One hundred dollars" was Barney's reply. The budget for our original plan was going to be zero. However, now that it was going to be such a public event, Barney pulled out all the stops.

The next day, I received a phone call. "Hi. This is Carol, and I'm your wedding planner." Wow! I couldn't believe my ears. We had a wedding planner! It was going to be a serious affair. After discussing a few details with Carol, Barney and I realized we needed to do some planning of our own.

We went on the internet and purchased gold wedding bands engraved with our names and "02-20-2002." We ordered bride and groom baseball caps with the "Bride" cap in white and the "Groom" cap in black. Barney located a decent-looking pair of black shorts in the closet, and I found a T-shirt online that looked like a tuxedo with a red carnation boutonniere. I added some tuxedo "tails" to his cap to make it look more formal and to protect his neck from the hot afternoon sun. He was all set.

Next, I went to the fabric store to get some white satin material for a pair of shorts and netting for my veil. I quickly sewed up the shorts and attached netting to my "Bride" cap plus some netting to my tennis shoes for that added bride look. Then I went to the mall to find a suitable top. There on a sale rack was a plain white T-shirt-style top with satin trim and little embroidered white flowers around the neckline. It had a small blue ink pen mark, resulting in a drastic markdown in price: $1.90. "I'll take it!" I was excited to show Barney what a great purchase I had made. The salesperson suggested using a little hair spray to remove the stain, and just as she had said, the ink mark completely disappeared. The final touch was a bridal bouquet. I made a quick trip to the local craft store for some artificial flowers, and I was done. We were ready for our big day.

On Sunday, February 17, we headed to Phoenix. Fellow pickleballers Mark Friedenberg and Pat Kane were on the same flight. After we arrived at the Phoenix Sky Harbor Airport, Larry Seekins picked us all up in a very tiny rental car. We squeezed in and headed to the Happy Trails Resort in Surprise to check out the tournament venue. Barney and I also made a trip to meet with the pastor. When we had contacted him earlier, he had agreed to perform our wedding ceremony on one condition: he had to interview us in person beforehand. I'm sure a wedding in the middle of a major pickleball tournament sounded like some kind of a circus affair, and he had to make sure we were a legitimate couple with serious intentions before involving himself. We passed the test, and with a warm handshake, he agreed to marry us on Wednesday.

Early Monday morning, before our first matches, Larry drove us (Mark, Pat, Barney, and me) to the hotel where my women's doubles partner, June Crabb, was staying. She had a slightly larger car than Larry's, so the six of us piled into her car and went to a nearby IHOP for breakfast. Almost every morning of the weeklong tournament, we would repeat this routine: Barney and I with our wedding entourage would have breakfast at IHOP, then dash off to a fun day of competition, winning a few awards along the way. Having June at the steering wheel guaranteed that we would get where we needed to be on time. She was known for her confident "take no prisoners" driving skills that sometimes had her passengers stepping on their imaginary brake pedals, but we would always arrive safely. That first day of competition, it was June's signature hook shot and quick hands at the net that helped the two of us win the gold medal. The week was off to a great start.

On Wednesday, 02-20-2002, we changed it up a bit. Pat suggested that we have breakfast at Sun City Grand, just a short distance from Happy Trails. As we walked into the restaurant, I could hear music playing softly in the background. I turned to Barney. "Do you hear what they're playing? It's the Wedding March." I'd never heard Wagner's Lohengrin played as background music in a restaurant, but this purely coincidental morning selection seemed to bode well for what was to come.

The mixed doubles competition began at 8:00 a.m. With so many players, it was a very long wait before we saw any action on the court. We won our first match and then sped off to change clothes for our afternoon nuptials. Promptly at 2:00 p.m. on court #2, the ceremony began. Carol had hired a violinist to play the wedding march. On the court was an arched arbor decorated with pickleballs and ribbons. We had to pass under the arbor to reach the spot where the pastor stood waiting for us. June, my matron of honor, and Larry, Barney's best man, stood a short distance away. The pastor led us through our vows, and after a few brief words, we were married. Cheers arose from the players surrounding the court. We were directed to go back through the arbor and pass the long double row of players, standing with paddles crossed in the air to form a pickleball arch. On the way, I felt a smack on my backside—one of the risks of passing through a pickleball gauntlet. It was all in good fun, but I wondered who had done it. Weeks later, when photos of our wedding were sent to us, I was able to identify the culprit: there, clearly pictured, was Judy Davis with her pickleball paddle in mid-swing. She had been caught in the act!

All the guests had cake and punch. I marveled at how $100 could go so far, but I suspect that the Happy Trails Pickleball Club dipped into their funds to augment our rather skimpy budget. Barney and I were all smiles. Married in Arizona at the ASO with two hundred guests whom we didn't know. Then suddenly, Barney spotted two familiar faces. His aunt Ruth and uncle Burt Liskey had driven over 180 miles from Lake Havasu City, Arizona, to attend our wedding. Not knowing the location, they had driven all around town asking at several places if anyone knew where the pickleball tournament was being held. When they finally found us, it was a wonderful surprise. We chatted a bit, but the visit had to be brief. There were still matches to be played. The announcer's voice had come across the PA system: "Next up on court number two, Barney and Fran Myer playing Beverly and Bob Youngren." In a gesture of good sportsmanship, Beverly offered to postpone our match, thinking it wouldn't be fair to compete against us right after our wedding. No need, we assured her. When Barney and I won the first game, Beverly said that was our wedding gift—but now they were going to get serious. And they did, winning the next two games and the right to advance to the next round in the winners' bracket.

ASO commissioner Earl and his wife, Gladys, hosted a wedding reception at their home after the day's competition.

There, we were formally introduced to many of our guests. Best man Larry Seekins likes to tell everyone that he paid us so he could sing at our reception. He whipped out his ukulele and regaled everyone with his rendition of "Frog Went a-Courtin'" with Barney as Mr. Frog and me as Miss Franny Mouse.

It had been a perfect day. We earned the bronze medal in our event, but our wedding was better than any pickleball award. Knowing that Barney and I would have each other to grow old with was everything. The entire day was magical, fun, and very special. Every time we recalled our wedding day, we would break into broad smiles and laugh. For years afterward, we would meet people for the first time only to have them tell us that they had attended our pickleball wedding.

Fran and Barney's 02-20-2002 wedding on court #2 at 2:00 p.m.

7

TWO NEW HOMES

Following our pickleball wedding, Barney and I made a point of entering the Arizona Senior Olympics tournament every year to celebrate our anniversary in Surprise. The ASO took place around the same time every year, so we were assured of getting in great pickleball competition while celebrating our special day.

When we were there for our first visit and wedding in 2002, our initial impression of the city of Surprise was visions of multiple retirement communities filled with nothing but old people doing old-people things. Golfers and residents rode golf carts everywhere, going to restaurant dinners at 4:00 p.m. during special discounted senior hours. What we saw missing was age diversity. Where were all the children and young adults? Also missing was the ethnic mix I had grown up with. No Asian eateries or stores offered Chinese goods that I was accustomed to getting at local restaurants and grocers in Seattle. Our plans for Barney to retire in 2005 and me in 2006 still seemed far in the future, so we really had no thoughts about what our post-retirement life would be like, but we thought it definitely would not look like this.

Surprise was founded in 1929 and incorporated in 1960 with a population of five hundred. The city is located northwest of Phoenix, 40 miles from Sky Harbor Airport. By the time Barney and I were making our annual visits in the early 2000s, the population had grown to sixty thousand. In 2003, the city of Surprise became the Major League Baseball Spring Training home of the Texas Rangers and Kansas City Royals. The growth of the city was greatly accelerated by baseball and many other activities, including a number of beautiful golf courses. The increase in snowbirds—retirees making their winter homes in warmer climes—added to the rapid growth of the city. By the time we returned to Surprise again in 2004, we could see the dramatic changes with a wider variety of stores and restaurants. The city had also built new schools in response to the rising number of young families that had moved to Surprise. A new high school stood across from the Arizona Traditions community where Earl and Gladys lived, bringing opportunities for retirees to volunteer and interact with the students. The city was quickly becoming more diverse and dynamic.

Earl and his wife, Gladys, hosted our February visits in 2003 and 2004. They were both active, energetic, fun people who participated in many different activities in Arizona Traditions. They showed us that residents of these retirement communities could be actively involved in golfing, hiking, playing bridge, swimming, playing pickleball, riding bikes, and more. We discovered many other activities to engage in while living in these communities. One evening our conversation turned to retirement and what plans we might have. Barney and I still owned our two houses. Having rental property can be a lot of work and we were ripe for suggestions. "You should sell your rental and buy a house here in Surprise," Earl suggested. The thought hadn't occurred to us, but it sounded like an attractive option. After we returned to Seattle, we gave it serious consideration. We met with our CPA, who suggested that if we planned to purchase an Arizona home and be snowbirds, we should sell my house, move to Barney's house for two years to avoid tax penalties, and then sell that house and purchase a condo. This would give us more freedom to leave for six months at a time.

With a plan of action in mind, we made a trip back to Surprise in April to see what lots or homes were still available in Arizona Traditions. During the times we had visited Earl and Gladys in this community, we had grown to enjoy everything

40

about it. Now, the thought of actually owning a home here seemed like a fairy tale come true.

We drove to the northwest part of the community where there were empty lots waiting to be sold. Barney selected the lot he felt would offer us the best location and orientation. Our house would have the front door facing west, providing a backyard shaded from the late afternoon sun. The lot was also within walking distance to the community's pickleball courts. It was a perfect choice. We had no trouble deciding what model house we wanted or picking out all the finishes and upgrades. Every decision added to the excitement as we realized that we were going to have our own dream home in the sun.

The lot we selected was #600, and we didn't learn until the paperwork was drawn up that the house number would be 18447. Only recently, I had noticed that every home I had owned had a house number ending in "7." Once we sold my house and moved to Barney's house, it also had a house number ending in "7." In all, that would be five addresses with a house number ending in "7." Since seven is considered a lucky number in so many cultures, we took this as a very good sign.

The house in Surprise was not scheduled for completion until the end of the year. In the meantime, we had work to do. We had to sell my house in Seattle and move to Barney's house while also shopping for a condo. Looking back, this all sounds a bit frenetic and driven by some unknown force. We kept moving forward like a couple that had no time to lose. Throughout all this activity, we kept going to our respective jobs and kept up with ever-increasing orders for Pickleball Stuff, while being totally immersed in the sport as commissioners for the Greater Seattle Senior Games and the Washington State Senior Games.

After working feverishly to clean, organize, and stage my house, we put it on the market in May. By June 11, we had sold it and handed over the keys to the new owner. That unknown force kept pushing us forward. In our spare time, we visited various communities around the Seattle area, looking at condos and townhomes. We spent time in their nearby shops and restaurants, taking in the ambiance to see if it felt right for us.

Heidi was pregnant with Barney's first grandchild during this time, and there was a lot of excited anticipation as the family awaited the approaching due date. In late August, Heidi went into labor and we were on alert for a phone call announcing the baby's birth. She experienced a long, difficult labor that lasted over thirty hours. The decision was finally made to do a cesarean section. As we celebrated the arrival of Heidi and Jack's son, Coleman, Heidi began to experience some very serious post-delivery problems that required more surgery the following day. Once Heidi's condition started to improve, we all breathed a sigh of relief and were able to really appreciate the joy of having a new baby in the family. He was beautiful and perfect in every way. I remember seeing him shortly after his birth, eyes wide open, calmly taking in his new surroundings and Grandpa Barney smiling broadly as he held his grandchild for the first time.

Barney holding Coleman on the day he was born

In September, we found our new Seattle-area home. It was in a small community of townhouses under construction, and the unit we picked was not scheduled to be built until the following year. The timing was ideal. Our real estate agent drew up the papers, and as we prepared to sign, I noticed that our new house number ended in "5." I felt a slight bit of disappointment to have my string of lucky number sevens broken, but we really loved the townhouse so, without further hesitation, we signed the papers.

The following day, our agent called. Due to an error, she needed to send an addendum to the Purchase and Sale Agreement. My heart rate went up a bit as several possibilities went through my mind. Then she explained, "The address on your agreement is for the model unit you visited. The address for *your* unit is 17817." I couldn't believe it. My string of lucky sevens hadn't been broken after all.

8

GARAGE MAHAL

Tiling was something that Barney really enjoyed. I'm not sure what he found more satisfying: doing the peaceful solitary work, creating beautifully tiled projects, or having an outlet for his boundless energy. No surface was safe from his impulse to tile. Once while I was in New York visiting Alex, Barney removed perfectly good vinyl floors in two bathrooms and tiled them in my absence. By the time Barney retired in March 2005, he had tiled the floor in four bathrooms, including the counter and bath surround of one. He had tiled the kitchen floor and counter, as well as the front porch and stairs of his North Seattle home. He also tiled the floor of the gazebo that he had built in the front yard of my house with the help of his brother, Ed. The townhouse that we'd purchased was almost complete. It seemed that Barney had tiled everything possible by then.

"I've got a great idea for your next project," I said to him one day. "Why don't you tile the garage in our new townhouse?"

Most husbands would laugh this off as a crazy, ridiculous idea. But Barney gave an enthusiastic response and immediately set about sketching ideas and noting measurements for his fun new endeavor. The next day, he asked, "How would you like the floor to be tiled in marble?"

"Are you kidding?" I replied. "I love that idea!" Who's the crazy one now?

Soon, we were off to an auction event for natural stone tiles. Our friend Erne Perry and his wife, Kim, had told Barney about it, and they too needed tiles for their own projects. As the four of us walked around looking at bins of tiles, Barney wrote down the ones we liked and how much of each we would bid on.

Included in the auction were granite countertops, ornate marble fireplaces, and unique bathroom sinks. It was hard for me to resist the temptation to bid on more than we had planned. We decided on a beautiful light tan marble with which we would also create an area in the center of the garage bordered by travertine and accented with black granite. Once the auction began, we had to remain alert for the bins and lots we wanted and be prepared to make our bids. It was a little nerve wracking as bin and lot numbers were called and hands went up in the air. In the end, we managed to get all the tiles on Barney's list. There was no way we could take all the tile home in our small car, but Erne and Kim had a pickup truck and offered to take our tiles home for us. As we all helped to unload the truck and fill the back section of our two-car tandem garage, I could see that tiling the entire garage was going to be a major undertaking.

Over the following weeks, Barney worked tirelessly every day, measuring, cutting, and laying down the intricate pattern and also creating a vertical border along the entire inside perimeter wall of the garage. On several occasions, Heidi's husband, Jack, came to help. After the tiling was complete, it was quite a sight to see how the concrete floor had been completely transformed. The gleaming marble tiles filled me with pride and wonder over Barney's beautiful workmanship.

"What color do you want me to paint the garage?" Barney asked.

This garage deserved more than an ordinary painted wall. "I was thinking of using Venetian plaster on the walls and ceiling," I replied. Again, Barney good-naturedly indulged me in my suggestion, and the next day he was in the garage with a plaster bucket in one hand and a trowel in the other.

Once the walls and ceiling were complete, he installed crown molding for that finishing touch. A local lighting store was having a sale, and one of the chandeliers looked like it would be a perfect addition to our new garage. We asked to have it shipped to our townhouse. When it arrived two days later, we opened the box and discovered the frame of the chandelier and twenty-four little plastic bags filled with crystal beads. Assembly required. Not the least bit discouraged, Barney started putting it together while I went to a meeting. When I came home several hours later, it was already completed and hanging from the ceiling.

Furniture and decorative items were purchased, completing Barney's masterpiece. It looked absolutely amazing. At the same time, my daughter Alex mentioned that *Family Handyman* magazine was having a contest for America's Coolest Garage. I thought our garage was definitely too cool not to enter into the contest, so we asked Heidi to come with her good camera to take some pictures for us. Our entry was sent away and before long we were notified by *Family Handyman* magazine that Barney's garage had been selected as one of the ten coolest garages in America. A picture and description of it appeared in the September 2006 issue.

This was Barney's final big home improvement project. The scale of the project and subsequent recognition by *Family Handyman* magazine made it very special for both of us.

To this day, I love being in the garage, relaxing in one of the rich maroon-colored ultra-suede chairs with Italian music softly emanating from the stereo system, polishing the car (yes, it really is parked in there), or organizing the storage area behind the false wall. Barney touched every inch of this space—each marble tile, all the pieces of crown molding, and every tool in his neatly organized shop area. His creative energy surrounds me when I am there. The garage has been used for birthday parties, celebrations, and meetings. Visitors who enter this space for the first time can hardly believe what they are seeing. Just as *Family Handyman* magazine described, it is my Garage Mahal.

The Garage Mahal

9

THE USAPA

By 2004, pickleball had become a dominant part of our lives. We had been involved in our pickleball equipment retailing business for four years. Our Pickleball Stuff website featured a comprehensive list of paddles, balls, nets, and accessories for sale. It also included a list of places to play, tournament schedules, a history of the game, instructions to build courts, and stories about inspiring players. By this time, Barney and I had also been the commissioners for both the Washington State Senior Games and the Greater Seattle Senior Games for several years. We were completely energized by all the pickleball involvement while simultaneously still working at our regular daytime jobs.

At the 2004 Arizona Senior Olympics (ASO), commissioner Earl Hill called a meeting open to all pickleball players to determine if there was interest in forming a national pickleball organization. Earl asked me to take notes. My records show that all 30 people in attendance signed a list pledging a $25 membership fee for the start of such an association. More people signed the list after the meeting, making a total of 151 people who had interest in creating this organization. After the ASO and the meeting, we went back to Seattle and waited for someone to take action. For almost a year, nothing happened.

In January 2005, Mark Friedenberg and Steve Wong started talking about creating this organization. Communications between Mark and Steve were critical in getting things started, as they discussed elements required and next steps.

The organization was going to be the new reestablished USA Pickleball Association (USAPA). In 1984, Sid Williams* had formed the first national pickleball organization, then known as the U.S.A.P.A. (with periods separating the letters compared to the new organization with no periods). Sid was the first executive director and president of this organization and presided until the late 1990s. In the following years, Frank Candelario became the president of U.S.A.P.A. with Mark Friedenberg as vice president. Due to lack of time and energy on Frank's part, the U.S.A.P.A. languished and all but disappeared. Now, Mark was going to breathe new life into the organization and rebuild it from the ground up. He and Steve laid out the initial plans. Mark secured the website, and Steve started updating the design and features.

Soon, Barney and I were included in email conversations with Mark and Steve, and I also included Earl Hill. Our first meeting was on January 25, 2005. Mark, Steve, Earl, Lela Reed, Barney, and I met to hammer out the initial details. Subsequent meetings included a few more members. Board positions were selected from pickleball enthusiasts who had a variety of skills and expertise. By June, the USAPA had a board consisting of nine members, all from the Greater Seattle area:

Mark Friedenberg*—President and Rankings
Fran Myer*—Secretary
Lela Reed—Treasurer and Newsletter
Phil Mortenson—General Counsel
Steve Wong*—Website and Vice President
Barney Myer—Tournaments
Earl Hill*—National/International Relations and Ambassadors
Dennis Duey—Rules Committee (made official in July)
Erne Perry—Marketing and Promotions

There was concern that this national organization did not reflect people from around the country. However, since pickleball was still a relatively new sport, almost nobody outside of the Seattle area had the game's depth of experience or intimate familiarity with its history and Pacific Northwest beginnings. It was felt that in time, there would be more nationwide representation, but for now the depth of knowledge was of greater importance.

Meetings were productive and ambitious. Steve quickly had the new website up and running. It created public exposure, expanded membership capability, and enabled the organization to start sharing information. Steve included pickleball news, rankings, a photo gallery, and more.

Barney's tasks included composing a list of tournament guidelines that described all aspects of creating and running a tournament. He put together tournament templates and worked to establish sanctioning requirements. He also responded to inquiries from people wanting help with tournaments, often sharing event scheduling tips and planning details with them.

Phil worked on the legal paperwork, and on July 1, 2005, the USAPA filed its Articles of Incorporation. Before the end of 2005, the USAPA added three more board members:

Carole Myers—Memberships
Jettye Lanius—Newsletter
Norm Davis*—Training

In May 2006, Bill Booth* took over as webmaster. He expanded and added many features such as the Places to Play list, using information donated from my Pickleball Stuff website in addition to other sources. I could now just have a link from my website to a more dynamic USAPA listing where players could enter new locations and update information relating to each place. When I first created Pickleball Stuff's Places to Play in 1999, I had 32 places on the list. By the end of 2023, there were 11,885 on the USA Pickleball website.

In the beginning, the income stream generated by memberships was barely enough to support the growth and ongoing expenses. By the end of the first year, there were just a little over 200 members. Steve had initially donated the costs of running the website, but the current income was hardly enough to pay the ongoing fees. There were minor expenses incurred along the way that were also donated by various board members. Everyone volunteered their time and energy, and covered incidental expenses, in an effort to make this organization a success. At one time, Bill estimated that he worked sixty-plus hours per week on the USAPA. It was gratifying to look back and see that all the hard work and dedication had paid off. By January

2024, the USAPA had 78,766 members and a number of paid positions.

Much of the explosive growth was attributed to Earl's Ambassador Program. His army of ambassadors included snowbirds who took this sport from retirement communities in Florida and Arizona back to their home states in the summer where it was largely unknown at the time. Some traveled around the country during the summer months, introducing the sport to people in RV resorts and community centers. Within five years, there were almost 400 USAPA Ambassadors around the USA, Canada, and Mexico. By the end of 2023, that number had grown to 2,144.

Bill was a true visionary of the sport. He was quiet, thoughtful, and able to recall the minutest details discussed during past meetings. No matter what topic came up, if the facts were wrong, Bill would set the record straight. Bill was the one who first thought to create the portable pickleball net systems that have become so popular today. Making these sturdy, easy-to-assemble net systems available to players increased the growth of the sport by making any flat surface a potential pickleball court. He was also the first to devise tools to test equipment in order to determine their compliance with USAPA specifications. Within a few years, he became president, and when the organization was just three years old, Bill introduced the idea of putting on the first USAPA National Tournament. At the time, I didn't think the pickleball world was ready for such a thing. But as tournament director, Barney had his marching orders: plan and put on the first USAPA National Tournament. Everybody started to scramble. We needed a venue, sponsors, food, water, vendors, referees, registration forms, and awards. Barney and I had experience from being commissioners of our local city and state tournaments, but this was going to be an order of magnitude beyond any experience we had ever had. While Barney took the lead, it was natural for me to assist in any way needed, having worked together so many times on smaller tournaments.

Norm had been working tirelessly with the City of Surprise to build public pickleball courts. The USAPA was elated when the City finally made plans to build and have courts ready by November 2008, our target tournament dates. I designed and distributed flyers, which were also sent out with every Pickleball Stuff order. Right away, a couple of players signed up. I couldn't decide whether to be excited or anxious. It meant that the number of participants could well exceed our ability to do justice to this event. Then Surprise suddenly rescinded their agreement. The city's economy had been crippled by the Great Recession, and they were no longer able to allocate funds for this project. This sent the plans into a tailspin, and the USAPA pulled the plug. Instead, it was agreed to plan this tournament for the following year, November 2009.

It was a welcome reprieve. Barney could now go about planning without a frantic deadline looming. Jettye's husband, Bob Lanius,* had been working for several years on a tournament management program that he was going to roll out at the February 2009 ASO tournament in Sun City Festival, a community in Buckeye, Arizona. This annual tournament had grown over the years, and we were anxious to see how well Bob's computerized TPBTMS (The Pickleball Tournament Management System) would work. Once we saw the benefits of using such a program for larger events, we met with Bob and he generously offered to help us use it for the first National Tournament. We had meetings with a representative of Pulte/Del Webb, the developers of the Sun City Festival Community. They had to be convinced that hosting these large pickleball events in their community could be mutually beneficial. It was pointed out that the tournament would give huge exposure to potential home buyers, and we would have a venue that could provide the twenty pickleball courts we needed. Permission was granted and planning efforts went into high gear.

I went back to the drawing board and updated the tournament flyer, then set about creating the registration booklet and program. As planning continued, the topic of awards came up. We needed a specially designed USAPA National Tournament medal as well as special prizes for the Open Division competitors.

Hoping to get the group's creative juices flowing, I sketched out an idea for the medals and emailed it to everyone. Apparently, everyone was too occupied with their own tournament tasks to devote energy to artistic creativity, and the general response was "Great design. Go with it."

Fran's medal design for the first USAPA National Tournament

By now, Barney had been struggling with double vision for several years. The optometrist in Surprise treated it as a routine visual problem, easily corrected with prisms, with no cause for concern. Though Barney seemed able to function normally while doing most things, the condition gradually worsened, and everything he did required increasing effort with the passage of time. Barney was able to orchestrate much of the planning in the early phases. Other board members also took on various tasks like organizing the vendors, getting referees, setting up the courts, and ordering the PA system. Dennis Duey volunteered to assist with registrations. That was a huge help. It involved detailed daily input of information into Bob's computerized system. From time to time, we would ask Bob if other features could be included in his program, and Bob would create the changes—often within the hour. As the number of entries went over three hundred, we felt relief that there was now a large enough group to make it feel like a real national tournament, but it would also be manageable since we had Bob's program. Eventually, this tournament management system, pickleballtournaments.com, would be used widely by USAPA to list and manage hundreds of tournaments every year on their website.

When the 2009 National Tournament began, we had players as young as ten and as old as eighty-five. The final entry count was 395 players from twenty-six states and several Canadian provinces. Bob, Jettye, Barney, and I would show up at the tournament venue before dawn every morning to set things up for the day's matches. We were the last ones to go home after dark at the end of the day. Without Bob and his tournament management program, we could not have had such a smoothly run tournament. As it was, there were occasional computer failings, loss of power, and other minor glitches along the way. One day, the PA system went out, and I had to run up and down the path between the courts yelling for players to get to their next matches. On another day, the generator powering the refrigeration unit for the ice quit on us. But for the most part, it was a tremendous success, and Barney received many compliments for putting on a great inaugural USAPA National Tournament. Of course, it was the result of the extraordinary group effort by the entire board and a giant army of volunteers. With the success of this tournament, the board voted to make it an annual event. Dennis Duey and I agreed to be the tournament co-directors for the following year—and then also for the year after that.

Barney during early morning setup at the inaugural USAPA National
Tournament in 2009

Barney retired from the USAPA board after the 2009 Nationals, but he will always be remembered as the tournament director for the first USAPA National Tournament and part of the history of this event. Bill was absolutely right about the timing. The tournament created an increased interest in pickleball and propelled the sport to greater heights of popularity. Over the years, the USAPA National Tournament has become one of the most highly anticipated pickleball events of the year. By 2021, it had been renamed the USA Pickleball National Championships, drawing over 2,200 players, and was already in its third year at the world-renowned Indian Wells Tennis Garden near Palm Springs, California. Imagine that—the pickleball national championships at the famous Indian Wells Tennis Garden. That year, as I walked around Indian Wells, I marveled that in sixteen years since the formation of the USAPA, I was there, walking the same hallowed grounds as tennis greats like Novak Djokovic,

Roger Federer, Serena Williams, and Maria Sharapova—
champions of the Indian Wells Masters/BNP Paribas Open held
here every year. Barney would be amazed and very proud of the
enduring popularity and growth of this annual event that he
helped to create.

*By 2023, these individuals, including Pat Kane (chapter 6), had been inducted
into the Pickleball Hall of Fame.

10

RETURN TO RAYPA

On May 31, 1970, Peru experienced its greatest natural disaster. An undersea earthquake occurred in the Pacific Ocean, 22 miles from the coast near Ancash, north of Lima. The 7.9 quake and resulting landslides caused close to seventy thousand deaths and the destruction of many villages and towns.

Barney was a volunteer with the Brethren Volunteer Service at the time. In June 1970, he was seconded (transferred temporarily) to Church World Service (CWS). With his fluency in Spanish and bachelor's degree in architecture, the CWS decided that the best use of his skills would be in Peru to help rebuild in the aftermath of this devastating event.

Barney's first assignment was in Huarmey, a city near the coast. There, he helped teach the Peruvians to build Stack Sack houses. These anti-seismic structures were the invention of Edward T. Dicker, a builder from Dallas, Texas. They consisted of burlap sacks filled with concrete that were stacked to form the walls of the building. They were simple structures that could withstand deterioration due to floods, storms, or earthquakes. More importantly, they could use available materials and manual skills of the local population to create these low-cost, durable homes. With the help of Pedro Veliz, Barney got the project started. He then left Pedro to complete the rest of the buildings while he went on to his next assignment.

The Stack Sack homes were so durable that in 2020 I received pictures of them from Barney's friend Rubén Paitan. They were freshly painted and still providing shelter for many residents of Huarmey.

A partly completed Stack Sack house in Huarmey in 1970

Barney's next destinations were inland to the large village of Aija and then to the smaller subvillage of Succha. Both villages were located above the ten-thousand-foot level of the Cordillera Negra, or Black Mountain Range, in the Andes. The restoration projects included everything from road and irrigation systems to building reconstruction.

In June 1971, Barney transferred to Raypa, a small village located at the base of some large mountains about 44 miles from the coast. When the earthquake hit, massive boulders and mudslides rushed down the mountainside and wiped out the village. When he first arrived, the village's ninety families were living in lean-to shacks on their *chacras* (small agricultural lands on the slopes of the Andes).

At the time, the village was without electricity or running water. With the help of Rubén Paitan, an agricultural engineer, and Nora Passini, an all-around administrator, the three worked to rebuild the small village. The trio started numerous projects such as cleaning water canals, teaching agricultural improvements, and creating guinea pig farms. They had about forty projects underway at any given time.

Working in Raypa was a frustrating situation on several fronts. Understandably, the villagers were working hard to reestablish their own homes and restore the crops on their individual *chacras*. By rebuilding in the same location, the villagers would be at risk of being wiped out again during future earthquake events. But they could not be persuaded to move to safer locations. Another issue was the villagers' disinterest in helping with many of the common restoration projects, their focus being more on their personal situations. For Barney, it was disheartening to devote so much effort for the good of the village with so little cooperation from the collective citizens of Raypa.

One of the last projects the village leaders requested was a school. It was September 1972 and Barney's time in Peru would be coming to an end in December. Given the lack of community involvement with other projects, he told them that he thought it would be impossible. But the villagers pleaded and promised that they would work like never before.

The villagers and CWS volunteers identified a hill some distance away that was protected from falling boulders and *huaicos* (mudslides). They decided that would be an appropriate place for their school. The hill, known as Inchan, was covered by a cornfield and was donated by the owners for the school project. With the help of CWS, the requested water pump to get water to the top of the hill was completed. Then Barney left the village to get plans for an anti-seismic school building from the Peruvian Ministry of Education. His directive to the villagers, to assure their dedication to this project, was to make eight thousand *adobes* (mudbricks) during his absence. With doubts in his mind, Barney set about getting the necessary plans. When he returned two weeks later, he went directly to Inchan to assess the progress of adobe production and was astounded. Indeed, the villagers had worked like never before. Instead of the requested eight thousand *adobes*, they had made thirteen thousand and were working on more.

"What do you consider to be your greatest accomplishment?" I asked Barney on several occasions.

"Building the school in Raypa" was always his reply. He would then recall the experience, always filled with great emotion in the retelling of the story. It was hard for me to understand the full meaning of his experience. I could feel the great affection he had for the people in this village and the close brotherly bond he had forged with Rubén. But his inability to tell this story, particularly his intense reaction to seeing the thirteen thousand *adobes*, without tears in his eyes and a break in his voice told me that building the school had had a profound and lasting impact on his life.

In 2007, Barney returned to Peru with his daughter, Heidi. His son, Eric, had been in Peru since February, working, teaching, and staying with Rubén. After reuniting, the four of them set out for Raypa. Barney was excited to show Heidi and Eric the village that he and Rubén had worked so hard to restore and to introduce them to the people whose families they had worked alongside.

Driving to Raypa along the bumpy, dry riverbed, they didn't know what to expect. There was no way to contact the villagers to let them know they were coming. As they approached Raypa, they were spellbound. The families who had refused to leave their lean-to shacks back in 1971 had relocated around the school on the hill called Inchan. The cornfield that originally held only the four school buildings was now home to over a hundred families. Around the school was a town with lights, running water, stores, a church, a health clinic, some municipal buildings, and a beautiful plaza that Barney had designed but which had not yet been built when he left in 1972. Raypa had developed into a complete town, alive and growing.

Suddenly, they spotted a large sign over the main entry of the school.

"Did you know about this?" asked Heidi and Eric. It was a complete surprise. The villagers had named the school in Barney's honor. If Barney had not returned to Raypa, he never would have known about this amazing tribute. It was an emotional homecoming to find that the people of Raypa had remembered him in such an extraordinary way.

Almost immediately, people started coming out of nowhere to greet their special guests. Barney and Rubén recognized many of them right away. They started to tell the story of how the school was named. In 2004, the village had a meeting to name the school. Several names were put forth. Some were of people who had passed away. And then there was Barney. After much discussion, it was decided that they would name the school in Barney's honor. Back in 1972, nobody had bothered to write down any of the details of building the school, and they did not know how to contact Barney, so they basically made up a history. Now they had both Rubén and Barney in person to set the record straight.

The villagers quickly began making arrangements for celebrations, school programs, and special meals. The guests were given tours of the school and were gifted with soccer shirts and badges and shown letterhead and banners. All items proudly displayed the school's name along with the logo: a picture of Barney's balding head and his signature mustache.

They stayed in the town that night, sleeping at the health clinic. The next day was filled with school programs, meetings, and ceremonies. The school had grown to twenty-two teachers, and they worked overnight with the students to put on a program for their honored guests.

The townspeople had also prepared a *pachamanca* to celebrate the visit from Rubén, Barney, Eric, and Heidi. This traditional Peruvian dish is prepared by digging a hole in the ground—an earthen oven with the addition of hot stones for cooking. The *pachamanca* usually contains various meats like lamb, pork, chicken, or guinea pig. Potatoes, corn, beans, and root vegetables are also added. Local herbs season all the ingredients, making a delicious meal. The tremendous heartfelt effort put forth by the residents of this little town showed their genuine appreciation for all that Barney and Rubén had done and the happiness they felt for their return. It gave Barney great satisfaction to see that the efforts of the villagers had developed into a town that was successful and thriving. The school in a corn patch was now the center of activity with expanded facilities and services, making it the best village in the valley.

Barney, Heidi, Eric, and Rubén departed for Lima the following day, still in awe of the experiences during the previous two days. In his journal, Barney recounted details of the unbelievable course of events, still shaking his head in wonderment. What a story he had to tell when he returned to Seattle.

Barney with Rubén Paitan in front of the Barner Myer School in 2007

One item of curiosity that nobody was able to address was the obvious misspelling of Barney in the naming of the school. There was no question about who they were honoring, but the naming of La Institución Educativa Escuela 86058 Barner Myer was a question that would not be answered for ten years.

11

SOMETHING IS WRONG

When a serious illness begins, often you don't know. Sometimes months or years go by before it's figured out. In the fall of 2006, Barney and I set out on a road trip to spend the first winter of our retirement in Surprise, Arizona. Our schedules were no longer tied to our jobs. We could hardly believe our lives now, with a newly built home in the land of sunshine and so many outdoor activities for us to enjoy. We played pickleball almost every day. We had fun meeting other residents of our new community, made many new friends, and enjoyed visits with fellow snowbirds from Washington.

One task that occupied a lot of time during the first winter in Surprise was furnishing our new home. We made numerous trips to local furniture stores and found many items at one store in particular. During one visit to that store, we noticed they were having a drawing for store prizes. Without much thought, we each filled out entry slips and went on our way. Several weeks later, Barney received a phone call from that store. They were notifying him that he had been selected as the grand prize winner of their drawing! The prize was a $1,000 gift certificate to purchase anything in their store. The caller asked if I was available, so Barney handed the phone to me. They told me that I had been selected to receive their second prize of a $500 gift certificate! We couldn't believe our luck. Several days later, we were back at the store to pick out our prizes. Barney selected a beautiful wood television stand with cabinets below. That completed all the items that we needed. I couldn't think of anything else to add to our furnishings until I spotted a huge, ten-foot-tall artificial tree. It was just the thing to accent our vaulted-ceiling living room space. I would never consider spending that much for an artificial plant, but it seemed like the perfect touch for our home. Barney loved telling visitors our tale of winning the store drawing. What better story of thrift than to get something for free?

Our first winter in Surprise was everything we hoped it would be. It really was like being on vacation every day. One day in February 2007, as we were driving down Bell Road, Barney casually mentioned that he was seeing double. Several weeks later, he had an appointment with a local optometrist and was fitted with prisms, eyeglasses for people who see double. That seemed to solve the problem.

In the months that followed, Barney's double vision kept changing. There were moments when things would look normal, then quickly return to being double again. It was not debilitating, so we treated it like a minor vision problem. We went to various optometrists trying to find a lasting solution, and in the process acquired several prisms of different strengths. Through 2007, he continued to enjoy playing pickleball, hiking, and other outdoor activities. He did his part in running our Pickleball Stuff business as he always had, being the shipping room guy who packaged orders of paddles, balls, nets, and grips. He would call customers whose payments were past due. At the end of the day, we would sit at our respective desks in the office. I would put invoices together with the day's payments and Barney would add up the checks and prepare the bank deposit. Every month, he would take inventory of our entire list of supplies, counting every ball, paddle, net, and grip. That summer, he was able to enjoy his trip to Peru with Heidi and Eric. Life did not seem to be that different.

By 2008, I started to notice subtle changes in Barney's personality. He had minor thinking difficulties. He began using inappropriate words to describe things, like saying "stilts" for crutches, "fireplace" for barbecue, and "glasses" for contact lenses. These were not unlike brain glitches that people get from time to time, but for him, it was unusual. Normally very self-confident, he began to express a little insecurity. Then insecurity gave way to suspicion. Eventually, he began accusing me of disagreeing with everything he said. At that point, I tried agreeing with everything just to avoid conflict. One day, while we were driving past a local coffee shop that also had a drive-up window,

Barney said, "I don't see why anyone would go to the drive-up window to get coffee."

I replied, "Well, I could see that if somebody was in a hurry."

Immediately, he said, "There you go disagreeing with me again!"

Feeling a little trapped in a situation where expressing my thoughts was now making Barney feel upset, I wondered out loud if our relationship might benefit from a little tune-up. I suggested that perhaps I could learn how to communicate better by visiting with a therapist or counselor. If Barney felt the same, maybe he could choose someone that he felt comfortable with, for us to visit together. He agreed and soon we were off to see a relationship counselor that Barney knew. I was relieved because I was certain that Barney was in the beginning stages of some sort of neurological disorder—perhaps dementia or even Alzheimer's. I was hoping for some answers and maybe even suggestions for treatment. We had several appointments, and the counseling was very helpful. Barney was open to the counselor's suggestions and took them all to heart. He never complained of my disagreeing again and conversations resumed without the earlier conflicts. I was relieved about that, but I was disappointed that I could not extract a recommendation for Barney to visit a neurologist or some other specialist who could medically evaluate his brain function.

I had no idea if the slight personality changes were even related to his eye problems, but little changes seemed to be happening to his personality and eyesight with increasing frequency. He was starting to become frustrated by his double vision and, after he hit a parked SUV, I wondered if it was impairing his driving.

Barney's frustration began coupling with a little confusion in 2009. His father passed away in January, and in February we flew from Arizona to Wenatchee for the memorial service. Years later, family members would recall noticing that Barney was not quite himself.

After returning to our winter home in Surprise, I expressed to Barney my own frustration and sadness at "missing my Barney." It was clear to me that he was not himself at this point. He shared the sentiment that he also missed the "old Barney." Finally, he agreed that I should make him an appointment with a highly regarded neurologist at Scottsdale's Mayo Clinic.

We spent the better part of a day there. When first checking in, we were given a personalized schedule that the clinic called an "itinerary," as if we were going on a wonderful trip to some exotic destination. It was quite a journey. Barney was interviewed, then given a complete battery of tests that included brain scans, blood tests, psychological evaluations, and EEGs. In the end, everything was found to be within the normal range and no significant abnormalities could be found. Due to the obvious visual problems, it was recommended that Barney stop driving. For most, being able to drive provides great independence and freedom. Barney didn't want to give it up. But on May 31, after we returned to Washington, he hit another parked car and finally put his car keys away. There was no arguing or emotional outburst. He simply realized that it was not safe for him to be driving. That was the last day he would ever drive.

During our five months back in Seattle from May to October, we were on a mission to help Barney. Desperate to find the cause of his difficulties, as soon as we arrived home in Washington, we made an appointment with a physician well known for integrating conventional, alternative, and nature-pathic approaches to medicine. We hoped he would find a cause that may have been overlooked by the Mayo Clinic. The following month in June, we visited a therapist who assigned eye exercises to help with the double vision.

In between eye therapy sessions, dental appointments, and meetings with the USAPA to plan the National Tournament, we maintained our busy schedules as commissioners for the Northwest Senior Games and Washington State Senior Games pickleball events. We traveled to New York and participated in the Empire State Senior Games. We also helped with two USAPA tournaments held at the SeaTac Community Center. In August, we both participated in a pickleball tournament in Port Angeles, Washington. Mark Friedenberg was aware of Barney's visual struggles and invited him to partner with him in the men's doubles event. Barney was reluctant because he realized how his pickleball abilities had declined. After much encouragement from Mark, Barney finally agreed. The results were disappointing. Barney was completely discouraged and depressed by his inability to do the thing he loved so much and had enjoyed for so long.

We didn't know it then, but that would be Barney's last time to compete in a tournament. In October, armed with naturopathic treatments and an assortment of dietary supplements, we returned to our Arizona home for the winter. Even though Barney had been working hard throughout the year to prepare for the USAPA National Tournament, it was a huge challenge. By now, double vision, loss of depth perception, and accompanying loss of balance were making it harder for him to function.

Though Barney could cognitively process everything and reason normally, he felt that his brain was working more slowly, causing responses to questions to take longer than usual. Taking a simple walk required great concentration to avoid tripping and falling.

After the work of the tournament ended, Barney's condition seemed to deteriorate further. Social gatherings were no longer enjoyable because he found it increasingly difficult to participate in conversations, play cards, or deal with the dizzying distractions of lights and sounds. A follow-up visit with the neurologist at the Mayo Clinic still did not reveal any cause for Barney's problems. Again, tests showed that he was within the normal range on all results. I was in total disbelief. It was discouraging, frustrating, and disheartening. Something was wrong and we all knew it.

12

DIAGNOSIS

In January 2010, Barney's brother, Ed, a family medicine physician, attended a medical conference in Seattle. Shortly after, he called and said he had met a neuro-ophthalmologist at that conference. "I think you should see him," he told Barney. By now, we were both so frustrated by not knowing the cause of Barney's difficulties that we immediately booked a flight to Seattle.

In Seattle, I arranged for Barney to see a therapist, who gave him a list of exercises to strengthen his neuroplasticity and neural pathways. We returned for a follow-up visit with the conventional/alternative doctor we had seen the previous May. Then we made our way to the neuro-ophthalmologist's office. After we shared a bit of background information with the doctor, he took out a cylinder with black-and-white patterns. Spinning the cylinder, he asked Barney to follow it with his eyes—up, down, left, right. Then he stopped. "I think Barney has progressive supranuclear palsy," he said. The doctor's aunt had this illness, and he recognized the symptoms almost immediately. "When you get back to Arizona, check with your neurologist and see what he thinks."

Somewhat relieved to finally have a name for Barney's collective symptoms, we didn't have enough information to fully appreciate the gravity of the diagnosis. Even Ed, in all his years of practicing medicine, had never heard of it. A preliminary internet search provided a sobering, grim description and outlook. "Progressive supranuclear palsy (PSP) is an uncommon degenerative neurological disorder that causes progressive impairment of balance and walking; impaired eye movement; abnormal muscle tone, and speech difficulties; difficulties and problems related to swallowing and eating. Affected individuals frequently experience personality changes and cognitive impairment." "No cure." "Nothing can be done to stop PSP gradually worsening." "The average life expectancy for someone with PSP is around six or seven years from when their symptoms start." My heart sank. The symptoms had started in 2007, and the six or seven years were now only three or four years away.

After returning to Arizona, we visited the neurologist at the Mayo Clinic. We shared the neuro-ophthalmologist's opinion. By now, Barney's symptoms had progressed to a point that made it easier for the doctor to verify the diagnosis of PSP. There were no treatments to prescribe. We went home somewhat in a state of shock, not sure what the future would hold. We just knew it wasn't going to be good.

13

LIVING WITH PSP

When I was a kid, I loved playing games with my brother, Fred. He was just two and a half years older, a quiet child with an acquiescent personality. We would play cards and the usual board games like Monopoly, checkers, horse racing, and roulette. Well, maybe those weren't the usual childhood games, but they did provide hours of entertainment. I recall one day when we were playing a pencil game. Fred, seeing that he would probably lose, announced, "I give up."

I quickly replied, "Well, I'm not a giver upper!"

If ever there was a time not to be a giver upper, now was the time. PSP was a tough diagnosis, but neither Barney nor I were the type to give up or give in. It was an unspoken agreement. We were going to enjoy life and at the same time find ways to stay strong and keep going for as long as possible.

Barney was willing to try many of the different treatments that were suggested as possible ways to improve his health and quality of life. Friends who had researched different cures for their own issues made recommendations. We looked for alternative medicine therapies and homeopathic remedies. Ed shared articles and news about treatments he thought might be helpful. We signed up for Atlas Orthogonal Chiropractic and therapeutic massage sessions. We tried acupuncture. The conventional/alternative doctor thought there was the possibility of Lyme disease, so Barney had a long course of antibiotics. We visited a hypnotherapist in Arizona to try to relieve some of Barney's anxiety. We made an appointment with a Qigong master in California and a spiritual healer in Washington. We both had Energy Enhancement System (EESystem) treatments and biophoton light therapy. With doctors unable to prescribe any treatment to improve or cure this condition, we felt there was nothing to lose in trying.

There was life to be lived, and I sought to help Barney make the most of the time he still had. He never expressed any self-pity, nor did he wonder why PSP had happened to him. Instead, he embraced all the exercises with determination. He was open to my many ideas for projects and recreational activities. He made every effort to remain as active and useful as he could be. His positive attitude made it easy for me to want to help him and care for him. Not that caregiving is easy, but Barney's resolve to stay strong and functional just made me want to help him all the more.

We purchased an elliptical and Barney worked out daily—and I mean every single day without a break. He was disciplined and motivated to keep up his strength. After each hour-long session, he would be dripping in sweat. He kept track of his daily progress on a spreadsheet, and though he would note periodic declines in pace or caloric output, he persisted with this daily routine for the better part of his illness.

While Barney's eyesight was a constant challenge, he could still see well enough to do close work for short periods of time. We enjoyed hummingbird visits to our backyard in Arizona. I took pictures as they hummed around and sipped nectar from our feeders.

One day, I had an idea. On my computer, I selected several hummingbird pictures and made them larger. Then I removed all the color, leaving grey outlines. I asked Barney if he would be interested in coloring these. He had enjoyed artwork throughout his life, dabbling in sketching from time to time. Using colored pencils, he completed two pictures. Then he colored a couple more. Before long, Barney had created a collection of six very nice pictures that I thought would make beautiful notecards. "What do you think of making notecards from these and selling them to raise money for PSP research?" I asked. Soon, we were making cards and selling them. During the next few months, we raised over $6,000. All of it was turned over to CurePSP, an organization that provides information and support for patients, families, and physicians who treat PSP and other related brain diseases. Despite his many limitations, Barney's notecard project gave him the satisfaction of working on something meaningful and positive.

In August 2011, Eric and Molly were married at Westwind, a campsite on the Oregon coast. Barney was still able to walk on his own as long as somebody walked with him. At the start of the wedding, Eric was accompanied by his parents, Mary Lynne and Barney, on the walk along the sandy path to the altar. This was followed by the entrance of the bride, also escorted by her mom and dad. As Eric and Molly stood reciting their vows, the ocean waves and sunny blue skies made a beautiful backdrop for the ceremony. The weekend-long event included an overnight stay that allowed ample time for visiting, playing, and relaxing. While many of the younger guests pitched tents along the beach, Barney and I had accommodations in a rustic cabin. All went well until Barney needed to use the bathroom in the middle of the night. As Barney tried to get out of bed, he fell to the floor. The cabins had no electricity, so I had been holding a flashlight in my hand while lying in bed. After I helped Barney up, we had to carefully navigate the dark downhill path to reach the building with the restrooms. We safely found our way back to the cabin, and I was relieved that there were no more falls that weekend. Barney was determined to be there for his son's wedding. I was glad he was able to be part of the ceremony and to have this special time with his family and friends.

Molly and Eric.

L-R: Fran, Heidi, Coleman, Barney, Bryan (Sue's son), Sue

Barney had already given up bike riding, so I purchased a tandem tricycle. That way he could continue to enjoy the Burke-Gilman Trail near our Seattle-area home. It was a great way to enjoy visits with friends and family, sitting side-by-side as they pedaled along. I kept a Tricycle Guest Book and took pictures of each riding companion. I asked them to write a message to Barney so he could look back on their visits. It provided wonderful exercise and refreshed the senses with the trail's beautiful views of Lake Washington, the Sammamish River, and surrounding natural areas. Sometimes, we would create a challenge like trying to pass four cities in one 6-mile ride: Bothell, Kenmore, Lake Forest Park, and Seattle. Another time, we decided to ride 9.5 miles to a little Chinese restaurant near the University of Washington. Our plans were to stop for dinner and then return home. We pedaled leisurely on the way, breathing in the clean, fresh air and taking in the sight of Lake Washington's sparkling blue waters. After dinner, we headed home. When we were about halfway there, the sun started to set. Once the sun sets, the trail is completely dark. So, with no headlights to guide us, we needed to step it up. Laughing as we pedaled furiously to beat the sun, we made it home as the last bit of light sank behind the hills.

Eric thought that he and his dad could surpass our 19-mile dinner trip. He planned an epic trail ride all the way to the Ballard Locks 17.5 miles away, making it a 35-mile round trip. With PSP's relentless progress, each day was always harder than the last, but Barney was up for the challenge. More importantly, it was an opportunity for Eric and Barney to spend precious time together doing something memorable. Eric wrote in the Tricycle Guest Book that day:

> We talked about the lofty goal of triking to Golden Gardens . . . The conversations were varied of topic from reminiscing the worst injuries we've endured, to beliefs about afterlife . . . as we entered Ballard the Burke Gillman eventually ended so we continued on the side of the road. Taco Time called us in for lunch of burritos . . . We huffed it back to Kenmore sweaty messes, fully tired and proud of ourselves. It was truly an epic ride. When I asked him if we should do it again, his exasperated expression let me know this was a once in a lifetime event. So happy I could share it with you!

Their huge smiles conveyed great satisfaction in accomplishing their goal. I found it inspiring enough to post on my Facebook page.

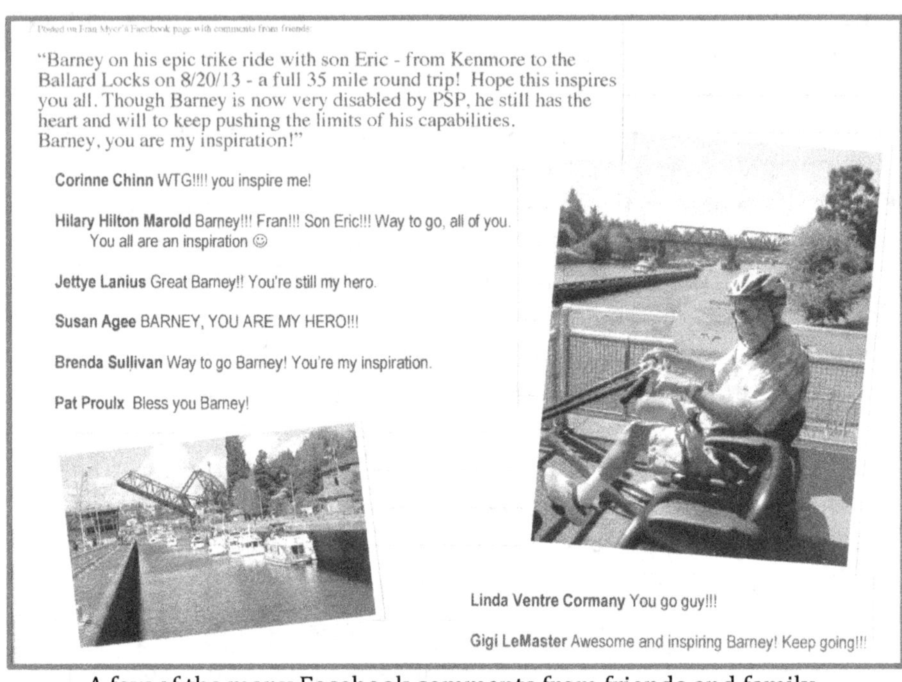

A few of the many Facebook comments from friends and family

The trike provided so much enjoyment for Barney that I purchased a second one for our Arizona home. The community we lived in had a nice flat loop road going all around the perimeter of a golf course, providing a pleasant trail for daily rides.

Barney, son-in-law Jack, and grandson Coleman in Surprise, Arizona

Barney had always enjoyed kayaking. I learned about a guided kayak tour in and around the Lake Washington shoreline near the Arboretum. It was a perfect adventure with two-man kayaks, which would allow Barney to have a companion to help him navigate. We asked another couple, Joy and Bob, to join us on this little excursion. On the day of the tour, Barney was helped into his kayak that he shared with Bob, while I got into the second kayak with Joy. I had never been in a kayak, and Joy was also inexperienced. The guys immediately took off while we gals paddled around in circles for a while, giggling as we tried to master this new skill. When we finally gained control, we were able to follow the tour guide and enjoy a relaxed outing on the water. We learned about the waterfowl, saw blue herons along the shore, and learned about the different features of this part of the lake and surrounding wetlands.

Bob and Barney kayaking on Lake Washington

By the beginning of 2012, Barney had started using a walker and quickly became dependent on it. Around this time, we engaged the help of an assistant to stand by while Barney worked out on the elliptical, to help get him in and out of the shower, and to offer any type of help needed. Danny Stickney, a licensed nursing assistant, came from a highly rated agency in Arizona. He was an angel with a thick southern accent and was an absolute lifesaver. He was attentive, creative, conscientious, and fun. Often, I would hear Barney and Danny in the other room, laughing hysterically over some hilarious videos that Danny had found on the internet. They would ride the tricycle together, and from time to time Danny would bring a delicious treat that he had baked at home the night before. This valuable assistance was paid for by the long-term care insurance that Ed had strongly recommended for us before we were married. It was a benefit that I was very grateful for.

Barney could no longer help with the business, so having Danny available to care for Barney while I packed orders and ran errands was a real necessity. Occasional incontinence and difficulty swallowing meant the illness was progressing to a new phase. With the exception of riding the trike, going out for any reason was no longer appealing to Barney. Watching the variety of birds that visited our backyard feeders was a pastime he could still enjoy because it did not require conversation or walking around. We delighted in the quail families with their tiny babies in the spring. House finches, mourning doves, Gila woodpeckers, and even pigeons would grace the walled area behind our house. One day, we heard Danny yelling from the back window in his Gomer Pyle–like accent. "That bird! That bird! That bird's eatin' that bird!" Apparently, Cooper's hawks loved our backyard feeders and visitors as well.

Barney always expressed appreciation for beautiful music. Often, after listening to a song, he would say, "I wish I could sing like that."

"Come sit next to me on the piano bench," I said one day. I had a collection of sheet music handed down from my parents with songs that were popular in their time. At first, Barney was reluctant to sing. Of Barney's many talents, singing was not one of them. He really did not have an ear for music. "You always wished you could sing, right? Nobody else is going to listen but us, so let's have some fun." With each musical session, his confidence grew, and soon we were belting out the songs together with my piano accompaniment.

Franny, Franny,
Give me your answer do
I'm half crazy
All for the love of you
It won't be a stylish marriage
I can't afford a carriage
But you'll look sweet
Upon the seat
Of a tricycle built for two.

Our version of "Daisy Bell (Bicycle Built for Two)"
written by British songwriter Harry Dacre in 1892.

Fran and Barney on a tricycle built for two

14

BARNEY'S FIESTA

The steady progress of PSP meant making constant adjustments and accommodations for the ongoing changes. It also meant broken dishes and damage to items in our home as Barney would invariably lose his balance and crash into things. Early in his illness, I replaced several glass-topped tables as a safety precaution. However, it didn't prevent damage or injury in other areas of our home. In one instance, he pulled the towel rack off the bathroom wall as he reached for something to prevent his fall. Twice, the toilet had to be replaced when the loss of strength in his legs caused him to make a hard landing against the tank, cracking it upon impact. A wooden chair and stool were turned into kindling when Barney crushed them in two separate falls. Several times, I had to call the fire department after Barney fell and I could not help him up. With all the increased falling, we were lucky that Barney never suffered any serious injuries and he rarely complained about any pain.

In March 2013, we tried yet another type of treatment. We had heard a lot of promising things about stem cell therapies and called a doctor in Palm Springs, California, who was using this new procedure with impressive results. It was quite expensive and not covered by insurance because it was considered experimental. Again, with nothing to lose, we gave it a try. Barney had had a pain in his shoulder for several weeks, possibly the result of a fall. Immediately after the stem cell treatment, the pain was completely gone. We drove back to our Arizona home, hopeful that other benefits would follow, but they never did.

We returned to Washington shortly after the stem cell treatment. I was sure that Barney would not have another winter in Arizona. The long drive from Surprise to Seattle was filled with many "last times"—our last time at the Harris Ranch Inn in

Coalinga, California; the last time at our favorite bed-and-breakfast in Ashland, Oregon; our last time to make this road trip together.

When Barney was working at Seattle-Tacoma International Airport, he had an office overlooking the runways. From this vantage, he created plans for the expansion of the Central Terminal and other projects while watching the daily takeoffs and landings of passenger and cargo flights. The progress of his illness now necessitated a move from our multistory townhome to a one-level condo. At this point, Barney's world had grown very small, and aside from outings on his tricycle, he now spent most of his time at home. While still in Arizona, I perused condos for sale near our townhome and spotted a unit that had a sweeping view of the north end of Lake Washington. Across the street was the harbor and base for a local seaplane company. From the window of that condo, Barney could watch the takeoffs and landings of seaplanes all day long just as he had when he was working. The location and wonderful views made this a perfect choice. After Heidi made an in-person inspection, we purchased it while still in Arizona. Heidi noted that the carpets were in bad shape, so I had the carpets replaced before we arrived back in Washington. After a little extra cleaning, we moved in.

The new condo was large enough for me to set up our Pickleball Stuff office and shipping room there. We quickly settled into our new routine, but we still needed a caregiver to help with Barney's increasing needs and to look after him when I was busy with orders.

We tried to find a suitable caregiver from a local agency, but they had a difficult time meeting our specific requirements. Once, while we were in between several candidates for this position, the agency sent a temporary helper just for one day. It happened to be the same day that Barney had gifted tickets to me for an excursion on one of those seaplanes he had been watching from our windows. There were enough seats for six passengers, so we invited my youngest daughter, Linda, her husband, Jeff, and Barney's brother, Ed, to join Barney and me. That left one seat. Take off was shortly after our temporary helper, an immigrant from Kenya, arrived. As we hurried to the seaplane harbor, we tried to explain to our new helper what we were about to do. We offered him the remaining seat, and without hesitation he joined us. I'm sure that wasn't what he expected when he showed up at our door that morning. As the plane took off from the lake, we were treated to expansive aerial views of Seattle and the surrounding area. The trip was exhilarating and left each of us with great memories. I'm sure the temporary helper had an interesting story for his family when he returned home from work that day. For Barney, one of his greatest regrets in dealing with PSP was his inability to help others or do anything special for them. As we disembarked, I could see that he was really happy to be able to give us this wonderfully unique gift.

Disembarking from the seaplane excursion
Back row, L-R: Jeff, the pilot, caregiver
Front row, L-R: Linda, Barney, Ed

One day, the doctor from Palm Springs called. "Barney, the stem cell doctor wants to know if you'd like another treatment." The first treatment had not had any effect on his PSP, so Barney declined. "Well, you're saving us so much money by not having another treatment that we could invite a few people for a party. Several parties," I suggested.

"Yes. I want a party," Barney replied. "A big party."

So, we planned Barney's Fiesta. It would be a celebration and an evening when he could see all his family and friends.

"I want a piñata."

"Sure," I replied. "Would you like a mariachi band too?" Of course he did.

I rented event space at the Burke Museum on the University of Washington campus and engaged a caterer. I searched the internet and found the most highly rated mariachi band in the area—Mariachi Mexico, led by Bobby Medina, a prominent musician and owner of Medina Entertainment Resources in Seattle. Heidi's husband, Jack, said it seemed like we were planning something akin to a huge wedding reception. Friends Wanda, Paul, Corky, and Jim helped to make hundreds of colorful tissue paper flowers for table decorations. Heidi and Jack planned a family brunch at their home for the day after the fiesta. It would be a weekend for everyone to come together for Barney.

On September 15, 2013, we welcomed a new baby grandson. Eric and Molly became first-time parents with the arrival of their son, Cyrus. It was a joyous occasion for the whole family, and Barney's spirits were lifted as we got acquainted with the latest family member. Barney delighted in every visit.

By now, PSP's relentless progress meant that Barney had to have an indwelling urinary catheter. As a result, he started developing infections. Late in September, Barney developed another infection. With his big fiesta just a few weeks away, we all worried that he might not be well enough to enjoy it, or even to participate. Another round of antibiotics was ordered, and soon he was feeling better again.

In October, family and friends arrived from out of town. Table decorations were put in place—colorful tissue flowers intermingled with little plastic Mexican donkeys. The piñata was hung. I had purchased a dozen Mexican-style straw hats for the family to wear. Barney was seated comfortably in his wheelchair not far from the entrance. As he greeted guests, I could see that it meant a lot for him to have this special time to visit with family and old friends and to celebrate with them. Guests ate, danced, and listened to wonderful mariachi music. They enjoyed the festive spirit of the entire evening. The positive effect of the fiesta was so much more than the stem cell treatment that I was really glad Barney had requested a big party instead. It was also a rare opportunity for my three daughters to be together and to be at an event with Heidi and Eric. Alex flew in from New York, Diane came from California, and Linda had a well-timed return from doing field research in Indonesia. Barney and I felt wrapped in their love and support. It meant the world to us.

L-R: Heidi, Eric, Barney, Fran, Alex, Diane, Linda

15

PALLIATIVE AND HOSPICE CARE

The glow of Barney's Fiesta had barely dimmed when he announced to Eric and Heidi that he was only going to last one more month. This threw the two of them into a panic. I was certain that he still had more time. To reassure everyone, I arranged an appointment with Barney's neurologist in Seattle so that we could all ask questions and hear the doctor's assessment of the situation. Indeed, the doctor said Barney still had about a year left and prescribed palliative care to help him deal with some of the challenges of his decline.

This triggered a steady stream of visiting therapists and nurses to our home. Barney was polite and cooperative, but part of him rejected the idea of trying to improve functions that would continue to be reduced by the insistent progress of his illness. Before long, he dismissed all the therapists and nurses.

Quite suddenly, in February, Barney announced that he wanted to go to Arizona. "Why?" I asked.

At the end of October, the refrigerator in our Arizona home had suddenly needed to be replaced. I'd made a hurried trip there and picked the most expensive model in the store. It had been on sale, but I had fun teasing Barney that I'd bought the most expensive refrigerator. "I want to see that new refrigerator," he replied.

I tried to figure out how I could manage to get the two of us to Surprise and care for him. With fingers crossed and a silent request to our guardian angels, I contacted our dear caregiver Danny and asked if there was any possibility that he could help us during those two weeks. He readily agreed. The two-week trip would not have happened without him. Ahead of our arrival, he stocked the new refrigerator, put out fresh towels, and made sure everything was ready for Barney, anticipating any needs that he might have. He met us at the airport and for two weeks spent all the daytime hours helping Barney. I was happy that Barney was able to have this last visit. It was a warm, sunny break in the routine, a retreat to our winter home, and a chance to see Danny and friends in Surprise again. We celebrated our wedding anniversary on February 20. It was wonderful to relive our wedding right where we were married twelve years earlier. At the same time, we both knew this was probably the last anniversary we would have together.

After our return from Arizona, Barney's condition got worse and it seemed that he was battling an unending series of infections. More frequent choking was another worrisome development. He had a steady stream of visitors. His youngest sister, Sue, and her husband, Mark, came from Spokane. His sister, Jeanne, and her husband, Jack, came from Wenatchee. All were painfully aware that their visit with Barney would likely be their last.

Determined to give him something else to focus on besides his deteriorating condition, I arranged for Barney to do volunteer work at a nearby shelter for rabbits and small animals. They had guinea pigs in need of socializing. The work involved sitting in a chair and holding a guinea pig for twenty to thirty minutes. Often, I would join Barney for this weekly activity. Barney had a calming effect on his little friends. However, my first piggie let out terrified squeals, then peed in my lap. Aside from that unfortunate introduction, it was fun holding these furry little critters—each one already named. One week it would be Alberto, Sally, and Alice. The following week it would be April, Annie, and Lela. It gave us time to sit quietly, just holding and petting these cute little guys. We noted the irony of how they would be part of a *pachamanca* meal in Peru, but now we were helping to make them more social so that they could go to new homes as someone's beloved pet. Barney's cousin Linda Haines came for a visit from Sacramento and joined him at one of his guinea pig sessions. I wasn't sure if the shelter had created this volunteer position just for Barney or if it was something they actually did with volunteers on a regular basis. Either way, I was

90

grateful for this wonderfully relaxing experience that helped Barney feel that he was still able to do something useful.

By May 2014 Barney was put into hospice care. A hospital bed was delivered to our condo. We placed it in the middle of the living room, facing the wall of windows overlooking the north end of Lake Washington. From this vantage, Barney was able to continue watching the seaplanes take off and land. On July 4, it was a front row seat to spectacular fireworks over the lake.

Though Barney could no longer work out on the elliptical, he was still able to walk short distances with his walker. Maintaining that independence was important to him. All along he had done his best to remain physically strong for both of us. To help him with some kind of exercise, I suggested that he stop in the doorways and march for fifteen or twenty steps as he went from living room to bathroom and from bathroom to bedroom, then back to the living room.

One day, when the hospice nurse made her weekly visit, she asked Barney how he was feeling. "Tired" was his reply. After reviewing his activities for the day, she told Barney that he could give up marching in the doorways.

Several hours after the nurse left, Barney made a trip to the bathroom. As he came out, he stopped in the doorway and started to march . . . eleven, twelve, thirteen, fourteen, fifteen.

"The nurse said you didn't have to march anymore," I said.

"I want to stay in shape," he replied.

Shaking my head, I thought, *PSP may be relentless in its progress, but Barney is still going to keep on fighting.*

16

LESSONS FROM BARNEY

As the end of Barney's battle drew near, we made plans. We confirmed that all our finances were in order and made note of medical procedures to be followed. Barney had decided to donate his brain to the CurePSP Brain Bank. It would serve as a postmortem confirmation of his diagnosis—the only way to know Barney's illness for certain. It would also provide tissue samples for ongoing research to aid scientists in finding a cure for PSP and other related brain diseases. Certain steps had to be followed immediately after death to ensure that the tissue would be in good condition when it reached the Brain Bank in Florida.

As we planned his celebration of life, I had an idea to make lapel pins with designs from his hummingbird notecards to give away as a remembrance. "What in your life do you want others to remember about you? We'll put those words on the lapel pins with your hummingbirds."

Barney gave it some thought. He decided on four principles that he had lived by, that had guided his life, and that would fit on the tiny pins:

1. TRY YOUR BEST: When Barney was a teenager living in Okanogan, he was hired to cut a neighbor's lawn. He did the job and came home. Shortly after, the lawn owner called Barney's father to complain about the shoddy work. Barney's dad marched him back to the job and made sure he understood that no matter what the job, you should always try your best. Moreover, whatever the task, you should always do *more* than is expected. Don't just cut the grass. Trim the edges and sweep up all the clippings.

2. HELP OTHERS: Helping others was what the Myer family lived and breathed. Barney followed their example with his work in Peru, as a high school tutor, and with his involvement in pickleball and the USAPA. I remember going with him on Thanksgiving to serve dinner to homeless teens. He mowed the neighbor's lawn when she was going through cancer treatments. Everybody in the Myer family reflected this in their work choices and activities. From church work, to teaching, social work, helping with worldwide health issues, working with communities to better the environment, it all followed the Myer ethic of helping others.

3. APPRECIATE: One of the many wonderful qualities about Barney was his ability to appreciate what life had given him. I loved how he would acknowledge even the smallest gesture or gift with a show of appreciation. I have saved notes, cards, and messages of thanks that I treasure. It is something his entire family does—always reminding one another that they are appreciated. It's a priceless gift one can give that can warm the heart of the recipient, because who doesn't like being appreciated? Appreciation can also remind you of the many things in life that are good. One Thanksgiving, Barney and I made a list. First, he wrote what he was thankful for. Then I wrote something. Before long, we had a list of one hundred items that included things like clean water to drink, enough food to eat, and having our children. I find that it always brightens my day to remind myself of the simplest things that I appreciate in my life.

4. IT'S ABOUT ATTITUDE: In life, one can have a positive attitude, negative attitude, helpful attitude, optimistic attitude, or any number of different attitudes. The one you choose is your face to the world and often affects the way people treat you in return. During my time with Barney, his attitude of positivity, determination, courage, and generosity not only influenced the effort

he put forth in everything he did but also inspired those around him to reach for bigger, better goals and to try harder. Those who have cared for a loved one know all too well how difficult it can be. Barney made me want to do my best to help him because he never gave up. He worked hard every day and showed great courage in the face of a horrible, debilitating illness.

Lapel pins with Barney's hummingbird designs

On Barney's sixty-eighth birthday, September 3, 2014, his spirit took flight. Eric, Heidi, Ed, and I gathered at his bedside and witnessed a peaceful passing after years of courageous struggle.

The celebration of Barney's life was attended by many. When Eric stood to speak, he asked how many knew his dad from work and various other areas of Barney's life. Several people stood for each group. When he asked how many people knew Barney from pickleball, I was stunned to see half of the celebrants stand up. They had come from Arizona, Montana, California, Oregon, and many parts of Washington to pay their last respects and to celebrate their fellow pickleball player. It warmed my heart to see this tremendous support from my pickleball family, and I was very appreciative of their presence that day. This is not to diminish the attendance by family members and friends from other areas of Barney's and my life. It was just so astounding to see the overwhelming support from people associated with the sport that meant so much to Barney and me. All the guests signed Barney's Tricycle Book, and when I look back on it, as I do from time to time, I smile as I read the messages of love amid reminders of the trike rides and adventures he had with family and friends.

17

A SIGN FROM BARNEY

Planners never die, they just show us new dimensions.

Before Barney's passing, he had discussed with Heidi and Eric what form his spirit would take after he left. Though he had grown up in a missionary family, Barney did not reflect the religious devotion of his parents, but he did believe in the possibility of some type of ongoing spiritual existence. "Look for a hummingbird," he'd said. It would be red throated . . . or purple headed . . . but definitely a hummingbird. Because Barney had created the beautiful hummingbird notecards, friends and family had come to associate him with those spirited little birds, and so it seemed fitting.

In the privacy of our last days, I said that I wanted him to give me a sign after he was gone. I didn't care what kind of sign— just some kind of *sign*. Something that would leave me with no doubt that it was from him. "But don't do anything scary," I said.

Barney's response as he looked off into the distance was just to repeat, "A sign."

Barney had decided I should keep our Arizona home. He wanted me to enjoy it after he was gone. "Buy a car down there so you won't have to drive back and forth," he said. After the celebration of his life, I found myself with a long list of tasks. Besides adjusting to life without Barney, there were many details to attend to. I had a condo to sell and a townhouse to reorganize while still running our home-based business. Each time people asked when I was leaving for Arizona, I would get a knot in my stomach and feel a bit of anxiety. I had to get the condo on the market before I could even plan my trip. There was so much to do!

Weeks passed and the condo was almost ready to list. Out of the blue, I received a phone call from one of my neighbors.

"What are you doing right now?" he asked.

"I'm in the paint store buying paint for the condo," I replied.

"How would you like to sell your condo to a good friend?" he asked. He and his wife were thinking of buying my condo. "Don't do anything else to the condo," he added. After a couple of meetings, an agreement was made. He told me that I could leave for Arizona anytime because he would take care of all the paperwork.

It was now mid-October, and though I had been looking for a sign from Barney, I wondered if this was it. It was a fortuitous real estate deal that was better than I could have imagined in terms of timing and ease of transaction. In addition, I no longer had to paint over all the repaired damage to the walls caused by Barney's falls. I was certain that Barney was working magic from afar.

Meanwhile, I was trying to sort out the logistics of getting to Arizona and buying a car. I had Pickleball Stuff inventory to transport to Arizona and boxes of files that I normally took back and forth. I realized that a better plan would be to purchase a car in Washington and drive south, so I made a visit to my local car dealership and bought my Arizona car. With everything packed, I began my journey on the morning of October 30. Ashland, Oregon, was my first stop. At the last minute, I was able to book "our" room at our favorite bed-and-breakfast. Though it was bittersweet to enjoy our favorite Ashland spot by myself, I wondered if this was my sign from Barney.

Later that evening, my cousin Roella called from Los Angeles. She had fallen down the stairs in her home. She was bruised and sore, but otherwise she was fine. I made plans to stop and see her on my way. She had picked the first fruit from her pomelo tree and said she would give it to me. Early on November 1, I arrived at her house and had a brief visit. I was anxious to start the last leg of my journey and arrive at my destination before sundown. As I approached Surprise, it occurred to me that I had forgotten my pomelo. The feeling of disappointment was quickly replaced with the relief of safely reaching my winter home.

Several weeks later, my daughters Linda and Diane suggested that we spend Christmas together in LA. I was delighted and looked forward to it. The next time I spoke with Roella, I mentioned our plans and said I could pick up my pomelo during the holidays. Unfortunately, she would be in London. "I'll give a fresh one to my son and you can get it from him. Here's his address and phone number. Call him and go pick it up when you're here," she said.

On December 24, I drove to LA. The girls and I had a lovely Christmas Eve dinner. On Christmas morning, I woke up early and made a quick decision to go get my pomelo before meeting my daughters and Linda's husband, Jeff. I entered the address into my GPS system, reviewed the route, and started on my way. I knew I was getting close and was preparing to turn, when suddenly the GPS voice commanded me to turn left. Too late. I shot through the intersection and had to correct course. After I made a series of left turns, the GPS voice said, "Turn left onto Barney Court." I wasn't sure I had heard correctly, so I looked up and saw that I was at the corner of First Place and Barney Court. I was awestruck, totally amazed, and then laughed at the humor of it. Barney's sign to me was *a street sign*! There were so many messages in this one sign. How fitting that the cross street on this sign was First Place. As a very competitive pickleball player, Barney had won many first-place awards, including first place in the 2008 National Senior Games with me in Rhode Island. And Barney Court—how perfect was that? We had met on the pickleball court, were married on the pickleball court, and had spent countless hours playing on the pickleball court. Barney had worked for seventeen years as a planner for the Port of Seattle. This was a brilliant plan. Starting with his suggestion that I buy a car for our home in Arizona, every step along the way had led me to Barney's sign.

I knew this was a Christmas gift from Barney to be shared. I quickly texted a picture of the sign to our children and Barney's siblings. "Merry Christmas from Barney," I said.

Almost immediately, I received a reply from Linda. That morning she and Jeff had looked out their window and saw a hummingbird. Right away, Linda had exclaimed, "Look—it's Barney!" The hummingbird made a loop-de-loop and then flew away. The sighting was made more unusual by the fact that they were staying in a hotel at the time. Just as quickly, I received a message from Heidi in Seattle. On Christmas Eve day, a hummingbird also had appeared at her window as she was wrapping her Christmas gift to me.

Astounded by this series of events, I sent the message thread to Danny, Barney's caregiver in Arizona. I received his reply: "Christmas morning, I opened the patio door, and a purple hummingbird came in and landed on my poinsettia on the coffee table. It just sat there. I picked it up and let it free outside. Before that I was thinking of Barney."

If there was any doubt that this was my sign from Barney, it was totally erased months later. One night while restlessly trying to sleep, I felt the sudden need to look up "Barney Court" in Hermosa Beach, California, on my computer. To my amazement, a map appeared on my screen showing that Barney Court is only one block long. Looking more closely, I saw that the street just below was another short street named "Meyer Court."

All I can say is "Barney—that was a great sign and I have no doubt that it was from you."

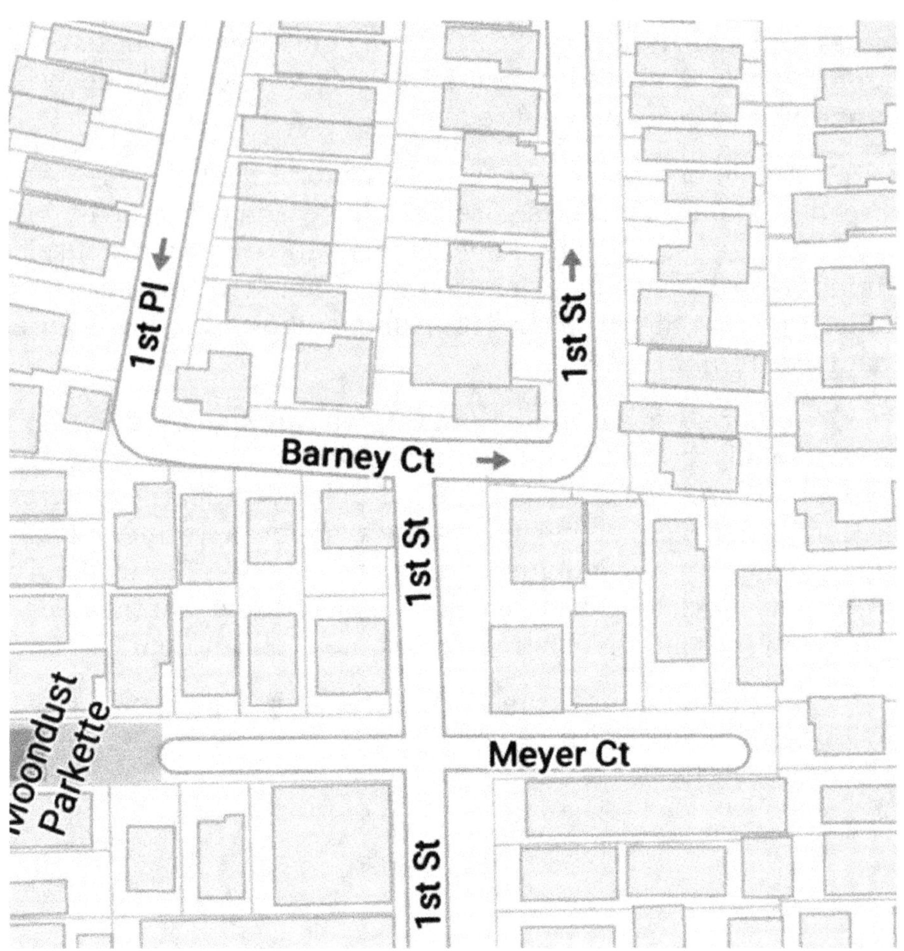

1st Pl
1st St
Barney Ct
1st St
Moondust Parkette
Meyer Ct
1st St

18
TO RAYPA IN 2017

Before Barney's passing, he'd wanted to make sure that a sum of money would be given to the school in Raypa after his death. Eric had reassured his dad that it would be taken care of. In 2017, two and a half years after Barney's passing, Eric felt the time was right to make the trek. Because he and Molly were expecting their second child in July, Eric had researched ways to get funding to Raypa without having to travel there. But Raypa was a small, remote town with no telephone service and infrequent mail delivery, so Eric's only option was to make the visit in person. He enlisted Ed to accompany him.

The end of March seemed like the best time, so Ed and Eric purchased their plane tickets and started preparing for their trip. The date was approaching when suddenly, just two days before their scheduled departure, Ed called Eric regarding news reports of horrendous storms, flooding, and *huaicos* (mudslides) along the Peruvian coast north of Lima. The transit route on Peru's Carretera Panamericana from Lima to Huarmey and continuing from Huarmey inland to Raypa was impassable. Their trip was abruptly cancelled and rescheduled for September. Everyone breathed a sigh of relief that Eric and Ed had just missed being caught in this devastating event that had killed more than seventy people and left tens of thousands displaced. Perhaps this was a sign from Barney, letting them know that he was looking out for their safety.

By September, conditions looked good for their travel to Peru. Roads were clear and the journey to Raypa was now possible. They were still feeling a bit nervous about any obstacles or dangers in making their way to Raypa. Eric and Molly had welcomed their daughter, Sabrina—now just two months old. Everyone understood what a sacrifice it was for both Molly and

Eric to have him away from his young family at this time. As was often the case since Barney's departure, Ed and Eric kept an eye out for positive signs from Barney. They hoped that Barney might indicate this was still a reasonable endeavor. After their flight landed in Lima and before their bus trip north, they happened to check the loose change in their pockets. What Ed discovered was a 2 soles coin for the year 2017. On the reverse side was the art of Nazca Lines depicting two hummingbirds. It looked like a very good endorsement despite some early logistical delays.

Front and back of the 2 soles coin

The bus took them from Lima north to Huarmey. A little over four hours and 179 miles later, the bus reached its destination and passengers disembarked. Eric and Ed had completed their first day of travel and made plans to spend the night in Huarmey. The break gave them the opportunity to walk around the town. They took pictures of trees in the park that showed the extent of the mudflow through the town during the flooding earlier in the year. All the hotels and buildings had been completely cleaned up by then, and all evidence of the incapacitating four feet of mud had been cleared out except for some telltale lines of the high-level mark.

The next morning, they arose early and went to the makeshift bus station on the outskirts of town. A bus to Raypa was scheduled to depart at 8:00 a.m. In Ed's recollection, this was the bumpiest ride he had ever endured. For about four hours, they traveled up the dry riverbed. Along the way, they hit some of the largest chuckholes he had ever seen, some about twenty times longer than the bus itself. As the day got warmer, Eric removed his sweatshirt. Underneath, he was wearing his Barner Myer School soccer jersey. It caught the eyes of fellow riders, who wondered about these foreigners traveling to their very small and remote village. Engaging in conversation, Eric and Ed explained that they were the son and brother of Barney Myer, for whom the school was named.

The bus arrived in Raypa early in the afternoon. One of the children quickly jumped off the bus and ran to the school to announce the arrival of their very special guests. As Ed and Eric got their backpacks and exited the bus, they found themselves almost in front of a very washed-out sign on the adobe brick wall that read "BARNER MYER." They were arriving without any prior contact and were not quite sure of their next step when a couple of young boys in crisp white shirts and little blue ties appeared. They were third or fourth graders at the school and had little logos on their ties with a machine-embroidered picture of Barney.

Shortly after the appearance of these two students, a woman in her early forties came out to greet them. She introduced herself as the *directora* of the school. She explained that she had been a student at that school decades before and had returned five years ago to ensure its progress. The *directora* had lunch served to them in her office. It was decorated with many of the students' art from a recent competition in which the school had won first place. With the promise to Barney in mind, Eric and Ed asked many questions regarding supplies and equipment and plans for the future. They discussed the school's library, technology development, and other ways they could help provide for the school.

Still looking for a sign from Barney and going somewhat off topic, they asked the *directora* if there were any humming-birds around. In Spanish, they are called *colibri*, but the *directora* referred to them as *picaflor* (poke the flower). She knew what they were talking about but said she had never seen one in Raypa. After lunch, she wanted Ed and Eric to survey the damage to the adobe wall caused by the storms and flooding in March. They walked outside to the far downhill end of campus. Along the way they were able to look through classroom windows and see children seated at their wooden desks. All were wearing similar neat white shirts or blouses, some with jackets, and the embroidered Barner Myer School emblem clearly displayed.

When they reached the location of the deteriorated adobe wall that marked the border of the school, they could see that flowers and greenery had grown up around the broken remnants since the flood. Suddenly, just six to eight feet away, they spotted a hummingbird sipping nectar from one of the blossoms and flitting around as hummingbirds do. Barney was there to give them his sign of approval. Hardly able to believe his eyes, Ed quickly whipped out his cell phone to capture a few pictures. Eric and Ed felt fully validated in making the trip and finished the day in the glow of Barney's appearance and blessing.

Photo by Ed Myer

One of the things they learned on this visit was the reason for naming the school Barner and not Barney. After the decision was made to name the school in Barney's honor, the school administrators had wanted to make sure they used the proper form of his name. They were certain that Barney was a diminutive form, just as Eddy is for Edward or Wally is for Walter. Having no resources to verify, they'd decided that the formal name must be Barner. It was a relief and also very endearing to hear that they had sought to "formalize" his name to properly honor him instead of merely making a spelling error.

At last, it was time to leave. They had a list of things that they could fund for the school, and Eric had made arrangements to transfer the money when he returned to Seattle.

Eric had brought along a tiny earthen jar with some of Barney's ashes. His original thought was to leave it at the school. Somehow, that did not feel quite right. As their visit came to an end, they headed toward Lima. Along the way, the bus made a stop a short distance from where Rubén lived. On the spur of the moment, they were able to contact him and arranged a brief meeting. After exchanging warm embraces, they spent a short time together. We knew that when Barney and Rubén had worked together in the 1970s, they'd forged a close bond. One day, they'd each made a cut on the wrist, united their blood, and said, "Brothers." Since then, they'd considered themselves to be blood brothers. As Eric prepared to leave, he suddenly knew that this was where the little earthen jar belonged. Just as Rubén had begun each of his letters to Barney, *"Siempre estimado y recordado hermano Barney"*—Forever dear and remembered brother Barney—the brothers were now together again.

19

BARNEY'S ONGOING PRESENCE

In the months and years that followed Barney's passing, family and friends continue to notice various signs. Whether it's a visit from a hummingbird or a well-timed odd occurrence, we smile to think that they are signs from Barney. He is never too far from our minds or our hearts.

One time, during a very challenging hike, Linda and Jeff stopped to catch their breath and assess whether they should continue to their goal. They considered turning around, when suddenly a hummingbird appeared. As it flew off, Linda said it seemed that Barney was encouraging them to keep going. Then the hummingbird returned briefly before disappearing from sight. That convinced her that they shouldn't give up. They managed to complete their hike, thankful for Barney's inspiration.

In May 2017, I sold the house in Arizona. Taking care of two homes was starting to feel more like work than the enjoyment I got from following the sun all year long. I had developed many wonderful friendships in Arizona and loved the active lifestyle. But, given the choice, my heart was clearly in my home with the Garage Mahal. After completing the final paperwork and turning over the keys to the new homeowners, I packed my car for my final trip from Surprise. On my way back to Seattle, I stopped in California to see Diane. During my visit, we went for a walk to browse through some of the downtown shops. In one store, I was looking at postcards, when Diane called out to me from a short distance away. She had been looking through a bin with a selection of signs, all with names of well-known local surfing spots. She held one up: "BARNEYS." "I didn't know there was a surfing beach called Barney's," she said.

To me, this was a sign from Barney that selling the house met with his approval. To ensure a safe drive all the way back to Washington, I purchased the sign to have with me for the rest of the drive. The following day when I started the next leg of my trip, I was unaware of a screw lodged in one of the tires. The "check tire" light kept coming on, and although I put air into the tire at every gas station stop, the leak persisted. It wasn't until I went to a tire store in Lake Oswego, Oregon, that the actual problem was discovered—and then fixed for *free*! The next day, I arrived home safely. I was convinced that my "BARNEYS" sign had prevented anything worse than a leaky tire.

In 2018, I was in Palm Desert, California, for the annual USAPA National Championships and to be inducted into the Pickleball Hall of Fame. My cousin Roella and my friends Andrea and Wanda, along with Wanda's husband, Paul, were all there to share in this momentous occasion. We were staying at a hotel with an outdoor courtyard where we met for breakfast each morning. The first morning, we noticed a little hummingbird flitting around and then landing on a nearby tree. We were all sure that Barney was sharing this exciting time with us. The hummingbird would fly to the tree and perch for a while every morning of my stay.

After my trip to Palm Desert, I was invited to visit friends in my former community of Arizona Traditions in Surprise. The ladies had scheduled pickleball for the Friday morning after my arrival. Unfortunately, the morning brought rain, so the games were cancelled. With free time on my hands, I called Carole Myers, a friend and former USAPA board member living in Buckeye, to see if I could come see her. She happened to be home, so I drove out to her house. It occurred to me that Danny, Barney's caregiver, had moved to Buckeye not too far away. Carole suggested that I text him and see if he wanted to go to lunch with us. Normally, Danny would be working on Friday, but he happened to be home that day and invited us over. It was December, and Danny gave us a tour of his house, showing us the many Christmas trees he had on display and pointing out the various quilting projects he had completed during the year. Then he stopped to point to a holiday decoration on the wall, which had temporarily replaced the display of Barney's framed hummingbird cards. Danny proceeded to tell us that his stepson had come by and wondered where the hummingbird pictures had gone. He was very concerned about putting them back after the holidays. Curious, we asked why that was so important to him. It turned out that his stepson was so inspired by Barney's discipline and determination throughout his illness that he had given a talk about it at his college graduation. I would not have known any of this if it had not been for the rain that day.

In 2019, I qualified to compete in the National Senior Games in Albuquerque, New Mexico. I was staying in a hotel during the weeklong event. One evening, I spotted a basket of small ceramic disks on one of the shelves in the gift shop. Each had a bas-relief of a hummingbird sipping nectar from a blossom.

I was compelled to buy two. I had no idea what I was going to do with them. There was nothing to hang them with and they didn't have any obvious function. When I got home, I set them on a console table that was filled with my collection of miniatures. Over a year later, still in their cellophane wrappers, I decided to examine them. The back was partially covered by two stickers: the price and "Made in Mexico." I could see that they were obscuring a message. When I removed the wrappers, the words were revealed: "I am Present." Barney was letting me know that he was with me.

We should not have been surprised by the intricate, often convoluted series of events that happened now and again, leading us to another sign from Barney. Planning. It's all about planning.

February 20, 2020, would have been our eighteenth wedding anniversary and the twentieth anniversary of our first date. Reflecting on what would have been twenty years together, it was hard not to feel a bit shortchanged to have had only fourteen years. After all, Barney and I were both very health conscious. Barney's dad and brother, our personal family physicians, were always there to reinforce good habits. I often told Barney that our goal was to celebrate our fiftieth wedding anniversary in 2052. We would both be 105, but I was convinced that we could do it.

Way back in 2006 as we prepared to head south to spend the first of our retirement winters in Arizona, a benign cyst, .5 centimeters in size, was discovered in my pancreas. At that time, Seattle doctors wanted to remove the cyst along with part of my pancreas. We were scheduled to leave, so I agreed to meet with a surgeon at the Mayo Clinic in Scottsdale for a second opinion. That turned out to be a very good decision. He thought rather than surgery, it would be best to just monitor the cyst for any changes. Over the next twelve years, things remained stable and there were no concerns. However, in 2018, the cyst began to grow. Again, there was little concern, and the plan was to wait a year and take another scan. By 2019, the scan showed that the cyst had grown to 3.1 centimeters, the size when surgical removal is recommended. An endoscopic ultrasound with fine needle aspiration was ordered, and after the procedure, I anxiously awaited the gastroenterologist's report. The following week, he called with the results. Though the scan did not show any concerning features, the biopsy showed atypical cells. I was referred to a surgeon to discuss my options. He turned out to be a surgical oncologist with Seattle Cancer Care Alliance. It was hard to keep calm with the cancer alarm bells going off in my head. The night before my appointment with the surgeon, I had a conversation with Barney. "I don't want to have surgery!" I said. "Please make it so I don't have to have surgery."

The next morning, February 18, 2020, I went off to see the surgeon to learn my fate. The surgical resident sat down with me first and answered a few important questions. "Do I have cancer?" I asked.

"No," she replied.

"Is there a risk that the cells will become cancerous?" I asked.

"Very little risk," she replied. She proceeded to show me pictures from the most recent MRI. As the different views of the scan appeared on the computer screen, one frame showed that my cyst was shaped like a perfect heart. Once the surgeon joined us, he showed me a drawing of the pancreas and surrounding organs and drew a heart shape to show where the cyst was located. "I think we can just wait for now and have another look in three months," he said. I was filled with relief, and as I thought about that little heart-shaped cyst inside my body, I was sure that it was my early anniversary gift from Barney.

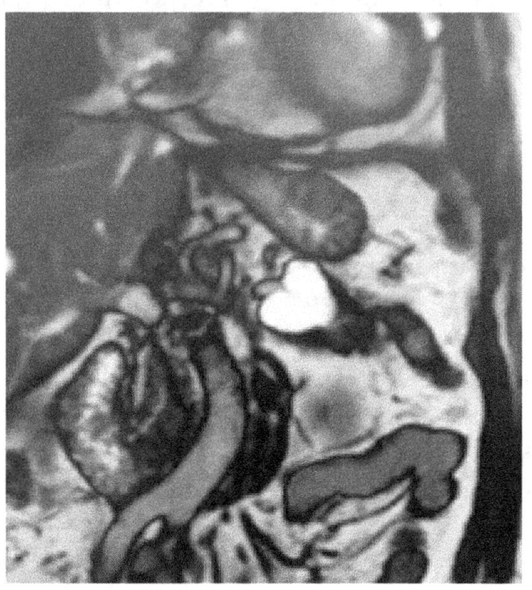

Then a tune returned to my consciousness. It was a song that had been spinning around in my head for several weeks. Every night, I was in the habit of using my smartphone to play something from YouTube to end the day as I fell asleep. A selection would pop up almost nightly. It was a song by Pentatonix, the a cappella group from Texas. I am a huge fan of theirs, so naturally I listened each time it appeared. I didn't pay as much attention to the lyrics as I did to the beautiful harmonic blending of their voices. The tune just kept returning to me throughout each day in a most persistent way. Although I had been listening to other music and playing different pieces on the piano, this song just kept coming back day after day for weeks leading up to the appointment with my surgeon. After arriving home from that appointment, something told me to listen to "that song" again. This time when I went to YouTube, a version of the

114

Pentatonix video came with lyrics streaming across the middle of the screen: "Can You Feel the Love Tonight." That was when the meaning of it became apparent. Barney had sent very special gifts to me for our anniversary. A cyst shaped like a heart and a song of love.

I feel a great sense of peace when I think of Barney's many signs. When I share stories of my signs with others, I often hear their own unique stories in return. They also are filled with the hopes and possibilities that our loved ones have gone to that better place and are watching over us. For the missionary couple who lived a life of devotion and brought Barney into our world, they would have had no question about that better place and the guardian angels who hold us in the palms of their hands.

AFTERWORD

Progressive supranuclear palsy and other neurode-generative illnesses are challenging for both the patient and their loved ones. I found the CurePSP website to have valuable, helpful information. The personal stories were also a source of inspiration. I joined a support group in Seattle that provided information about what to expect and how to manage various stages of this illness. Fortunately, Barney was already following many of the suggestions: keep doing the things you can still do, exercise, stay positive, do not indulge in self-pity. I connected with several caregivers whose spouses were diagnosed around the same time as Barney. We would email back and forth and share information about resources and communicate about specific challenges. One caregiver was in Alaska, another in California, and a third in Kansas. Having people to communicate with who understand your situation is vital because caregiving can be very lonely.

Pickleball became more than just a pastime for Barney and me. When we first suggested to the neurologist that Barney might have PSP, the neurologist said if that were true, Barney's case would be very uncommon because he was in such good shape for that stage of his illness. I suspect Barney's active life and daily sessions of pickleball had a lot to do with it, as well as his daily hour-long workouts on the elliptical. For me, pickleball became a great stress reliever throughout the course of Barney's PSP. The activity allowed me to stay physically active, work out some of the emotion, and engage in social interactions that kept me sane. I have long been an advocate of pickleball for the health benefits of staying active and fit. Now I encourage others to keep playing for all the ways it can improve your life, socially, physically, and emotionally.

Barney's wish was to stay home until the end. I am no Wonder Woman and there were days when I was completely overwhelmed. The long-term care policy we'd signed up for before we were even married was the life raft we both needed as Barney's condition worsened. It allowed us to hire Danny in Surprise and Rommel, the nursing assistant in Seattle, to be our in-home helpers. Barney's advance planning had enabled him to stay at home throughout his illness.

While I do wish we had had more time, I was able to look back on the years we spent together. Starting in 2000, I would end each year with a two- or three-page document that summarized what we did each month. When Barney was in hospice, I would ask if he wanted me to read a review of a particular year. During several weeks, we went through each year's summary. They left us breathless with the amount of activity we undertook and experienced. Often, there were dinners, events, and people we could barely remember because our schedules were so packed. We could see that our life had been very full, and there was no thought that we could have or should have done more with our time together. In that regard, there were no regrets.

In the years since Barney's passing, I have been able to allow the memories of his life before PSP to be more in the forefront than the memories of his struggles with this illness. As I recall all his accomplishments, travels, and adventures, it is clear that his was a life well lived. I hope this book adequately expresses a life well remembered.

Photo Source: https://www.deperu.com/educacion/educacion-secundaria/colegio-86058-barner-myer-raypa-97103

La Institución Educativa Escuela 86058 Barner Myer in 2020

Drawing by Barney Myer

Tressa May Burr Myer – Barney's paternal grandmother

Elizabeth Barstow Larson – Barney's maternal grandmother

Untitled drawing by Barney

ACKNOWLEDGMENTS

Ed Myer, Jack and Jeanne Davisson, Mark and Sue Agee—
Thank you for welcoming and accepting me. How lucky I am that
Barney left me with a wonderful, caring, and loving family. All the
credit goes to you, Jeanne, for suggesting that I write about my
sign from Barney. I had no idea it would become a book, but it all
started with you.

Heidi, Jack, Eric, Molly, Alex, Diane, Linda, and Jeff—Family is
everything. Barney and I always felt fortunate to have the best.
Thank you for your support, caring, and love.

Roella Louie—The strange sequence of events following your
fall down the stairs led me to Barney's sign. Thanks for suffering
those bruises, thereby enabling Barney to actualize his master
plan.

Mary Avery Kabrich—If any readers benefit from Barney's
story, it is because you gave me the confidence to write about it
and share it. Thank you for your friendship, inspiration, guidance,
and encouragement.

Earl and Gladys Hill—Your critical comments after reading an
early draft of my book helped me immensely. Thank you for being
such a big part of our story, for orchestrating our wedding,
hosting a wonderful reception and many fun parties at your
house, suggesting that we purchase our Arizona house, and
working together on the USAPA board.

Gayle Leach—"Thank you" is not enough. I appreciate the time
you took to read my early draft and to provide edits, and
encouragement. It meant a lot to me that you made so many
critical suggestions to improve the result.

Mark Friedenberg and Steve Wong—Thank you for your friendship and for inviting Barney and me to join you in creating the USAPA. It was a bold move that allowed many of us to be part of the lasting history of pickleball.

Sid Williams—Thank you for all the pickleball tournaments you hosted from 1984 to 1995. Without them, I might never have met Barney, and many players would not have had a way to test their pickleball skills in the early days.

Doug Smith, Janet Valentine, Barney McCallum, and Pickle-Ball, Inc.—Thank you for providing me with paddles, balls, and nets for my Pickleball Stuff business. I appreciate your part in the creation and growth of the sport that meant so much to Barney and me.

Danny Stickney—You are the best! Thank you for everything you did to help Barney. I wish everyone who needed help could have someone as thoughtful, compassionate, and wonderful as you.

Jean Sasaki—Thank you for your inspiration and collaboration through the years. Our partnership was wonderful, creative, and productive. All the experiences we shared provided the foundation for this project, and I didn't have to do the collating!

Andrea Deighton, Wanda and Paul Miyahara, Corky and Jim Kozu—To loyal friends who have always been there for me no matter what challenges I've faced. Your steadfast support through the years, despite distance and the passage of time, will not be forgotten. Thank you from my heart.

Erne and Kim Perry—I will always appreciate your loading all those marble tiles into your truck and unloading them into the back of our garage for Barney to create his masterpiece, the Garage Mahal.

Nadine Miyahara—I appreciate the time you took to read an early draft, provide feedback and comments, and your honest, open discussions about life.

Happy Trails Pickleball Club—Carol and Mary, thank you and the club for helping to create the most special day for us. You were the best wedding planners ever!

Pollard Dickson—Thank you for your friendship to Barney. Your input and details about the North Bonneville project were invaluable.

Jody Clovis—As a work colleague and friend of Barney's, you gave me much appreciated input.

Rubén Paitan—Thank you for working alongside Barney in Raypa and for your lifelong friendship with him. Our family's connection to you and Peru will continue to live on.

Harold Lewis "Barney" Myer
September 3, 1946–September 3, 2014

ABOUT THE AUTHOR

Fran Myer (née Jue) was born in Seattle, Washington, in 1946. She graduated from the University of Washington in 1968 with a BA in art. She began work at the University of Washington in 1969, then took time off to raise three daughters. Under her former married name, Frances Uyeda, she and Jean Sasaki wrote, illustrated, and published two children's books: *Chocho is for Butterfly*, and *Fold, Cut and Say the Japanese Way*. Fran returned to the UW in 1988 and worked there until her retirement in 2006. Fran started playing pickleball in 1988 to improve her health and physical fitness. She has over thirty-five years of pickleball tournament experience and has won over two hundred medals and awards. In 1999, Fran created the first online retail website, PickleballStuff.com, to sell equipment and supplies for the sport. Fran and Barney Myer were the co-commissioners of the Washington State Senior Games for nine years and the Greater Seattle Senior Games for eight years. They were also USAPA charter board members. In 2009, Barney was the tournament director of the first USAPA National Tournament (now known as the USA Pickleball National Championships). Fran co-directed this tournament with Dennis Duey during the following two years. In 2018, Fran was the first woman and first Chinese American inducted into the Pickleball Hall of Fame. She was recognized for her many contributions to the growth of the sport worldwide. She has written articles for *Parks & Recreation* magazine and *Pickleball Magazine*. During Barney's illness with progressive supranuclear palsy (PSP), pickleball was an important outlet for Fran as she balanced caregiving with running her online business and maintaining her own health. Fran believes in playing pickleball for the many benefits it provides.

www.ingramcontent.com/pod-product-compliance
Lightning Source LLC
Chambersburg PA
CBHW071323130726
47996CB00002B/600